50 CLIMATE QUESTIONS

A BLIZZARD OF BLISTERING FACTS

Peter Christie

illustrated by Ross Kinnaird

 annick press
toronto + new york + vancouver

For Hannah and Laura and every kid with questions —P.C.
For Hannah —R.K.

Annick Press Ltd.

Edited and copyedited by Elizabeth McLean
Original design concept by Irvin Cheung

We acknowledge the support of the Canada Council for the Arts, the Ontario Arts Council, and the Government of Canada through the Canada Book Fund (CBF) for our publishing activities.

ONTARIO ARTS COUNCIL
CONSEIL DES ARTS DE L'ONTARIO

Cataloging in Publication
Christie, Peter, 1962–
50 climate questions : a blizzard of blistering facts / Peter Christie ;
illustrated by Ross Kinnaird.

(50 questions series)
Includes bibliographical references and index.
ISBN 978-1-55451-374-1 (pbk.).—ISBN 978-1-55451-375-8 (bound)

1. Climatology—History—Juvenile literature.
2. Climatology—Juvenile literature.
3. Climatic changes—Juvenile literature.
I. Kinnaird, Ross, 1954–
II. Title.
III. Title: Fifty climate questions.
IV. Series: 50 questions series

QC863.5.F54 2012   j551.5   C2011-906966-0

Distributed in Canada by:
Firefly Books Ltd.
66 Leek Crescent
Richmond Hill, ON
L4B 1H1

Published in the U.S.A. by Annick Press (U.S.) Ltd.
Distributed in the U.S.A. by:
Firefly Books (U.S.) Inc.
P.O. Box 1338   Ellicott Station
Buffalo, NY 14205

Printed and bound in China

Table of Contents

THIS TOPIC IS HOT

NICE DAY, ISN'T IT? Ever notice how often we ask about the weather? Maybe it's because what happens in the sky matters to us all. Weather makes snow for skiers, rains out a baseball game, or delivers a perfect afternoon for a picnic.

Many people are asking about climate now too. While weather is the daily brew of temperature, wind, rain, or snow, climate is the weather pattern of a place over a long time, usually years. The climate of the Arctic is cooler than that of tropical Brazil, for instance. Weather constantly changes, but climate is something most of us count on.

2

But should we? Climate has become a hot topic because it changes too. While past climate shifts often took thousands of years, today our climate is warming fast—and people are the reason.

Change always raises questions, and that can be good. Asking what happened before might reveal what will happen next. A little curiosity—beginning with the 50 questions in this book—can help you understand why climate matters and what we can do about it.

CHAPTER 1

SNOWBALL EARTH and MEGA MAMMALS

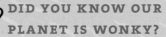

Hic!

DID YOU KNOW OUR PLANET IS WONKY?
It changes its path around the sun; it wobbles as it spins; and, under a gas-bubble sky, its cracked surface sloshes with liquid. And all of these weird activities have been shaking up our climate since the beginning of the world.

Climate shifts change other things too. The sky—its rain, its heat, its cold, its storms—can help or harm life on the ground beneath. New conditions mean that creatures and plants must adapt to survive. From bacteria to *Brachiosaurus*, this need to evolve has helped to create Earth's remarkable diversity.

Have you ever had gas this bad?

I'm exhausted!

Only a few billion years to go.

IN THE BEGINNING, there was a bad case of gas.

It's true: the world's first skies—and the first climate and weather—were created because our young Earth had a severe bout of planetary flatulence. About 4 billion years ago, most of our new planet's thin surrounding layer of gases—the atmosphere—came hissing out of its bubbling hot middle. Volcanoes filled the air with gases and steam. The climate became toasty because the gases, especially carbon dioxide, created a kind of air blanket around the world to keep it warm. Soon, it was downright tropical.

When life appeared, things cooled down a little. Bacteria and, later, plants evolved until they were sucking carbon dioxide out of the air and putting it right back underground. How did the early organisms perform this nifty trick? Using photosynthesis, a process plants today still rely on to turn air, water, and sunlight into food energy. The early organisms absorbed carbon dioxide from the atmosphere into their cells, then broke it down into oxygen that was released back into the air and carbon that was stored in their bodies. After the organisms died, the carbon was buried with them. Over a few billion years, this green team managed to stuff most of the airborne carbon back into the planet, leaving only traces still floating around—just enough to make the place comfy.

THE NEXT TIME you get ready to throw a well-packed snowball, you might want to stop for a minute and think about what it would be like to be trapped inside one.

Many scientists believe that's what life on our planet was like at least three times in the distant past. During "snowball Earth" conditions, our usually blue planet was all-over white, completely encrusted with ice thicker than the height of many mountains on Earth today. Beginning about 2.2 billion, 710 million, and 640 million years ago, each extreme cold spell lasted for millions of years. The ice and snow might have made for spectacular long-distance sledding, but early bacteria and plants struggled to survive, locked away from sunlight.

The big chills, say researchers, were caused by climate change. They were likely triggered mainly by changes in the gassy makeup of the air, as well as the shifting position of the world's continents.

The Nothing That Can Change the World

More than 150 years ago, British scientist John Tyndall passed heat through a small tube in which observers could clearly see . . . nothing. Only air was there.

Scientists already knew that air was made up of different gases, but Tyndall's experiments testing each gas separately showed that air's main ingredients, oxygen and nitrogen, let heat go freely through them. But carbon dioxide, a gas made up of carbon and oxygen combined, trapped the warmth. Even tiny amounts worked the same way as the glass of a greenhouse, letting the sun's light in while preventing heat from escaping.

A few other gases have the same effect, and they have all been nicknamed greenhouse gases. Drifting high in the sky, these invisible gases surround our planet like a blanket and prevent Earth's warmth from disappearing back into cold space.

TADA ! Nothing!

uh, oh!

QUESTION 3
Why is it suddenly so lonely here?

LONG GONE
Prehistoric global warming or cooling by as little as 5° Celsius (9° Fahrenheit)—the difference between choosing a t-shirt or long sleeves—has triggered mass extinctions.

THEY CALL IT "THE GREAT DYING," but scientists have long wondered what happened 250 million years ago that killed more living things in one fell swoop than at any other time. More than 9 out of every 10 sea creatures and plants and 7 out of every 10 land-dwelling species were wiped out. Now, researchers believe they have an answer—volcanoes.

In the deadliest event ever, a cluster of massive eruptions (possibly triggered by a giant asteroid crashing into our planet) flung so much ash and chemicals into the sky that the Earth became almost unlivable.

Back then, the world looked a lot different. The continents were all joined together in a supercontinent called Pangaea (pan-**jee**-ah). The landscape ranged from lush forest to barren desert. Primitive amphibians, reptiles, and other animals (including the group that would one day evolve into mammals) were walking about on four legs. The oceans were filled with strange creatures, such as giant ichthyosaur (**ick**-thee-uh-sore) lizards that looked and lived like dolphins and fish.

Change came with a roar. Researchers say a series of spectacular eruptions from volcanoes centered in present-day Siberia rattled the whole world. The fires incinerated huge stores of coal underground and ashy clouds rose to fill the sky. These plumes delivered enormous amounts of carbon dioxide into the air, say scientists, and the gas trapped the sun's heat, sending world temperatures climbing. Any life that survived the heat had to cope with choking toxic chemicals. Millions of years passed before the planet recovered enough for its creatures to get back on their evolutionary course.

QUESTION 4
Do you like my art?
It's from my blue-
planet period.

SOMETIMES CREATIVE PEOPLE make their most original art when their lives have become all mixed up. Nature can be like that too: periods of climate chaos have often matched times when creatures and plants were changing fast, adapting to new environments.

These intense creative periods, say scientists, likely happened many times during the billions of years of evolutionary history separating the first organisms from you and me. But one of the most interesting times was the heyday of the dinosaurs in the Cretaceous Period, which began about 145 million years ago.

Researchers say world temperatures were all over the map during this period. The amount of carbon dioxide in the air was up and down, but mostly up, causing temperatures to soar. A lot of volcanoes blew their tops too, and shifting landmasses pushed huge mountain ranges into existence.

Dinosaurs had to change with the times or disappear, leading to an explosion in the variety of these great beasts. Soon, almost every animal bigger than a dog was some sort of dinosaur, and the super-stompers ruled: ferocious *Tyrannosaurus rex*, three-horned *Triceratops*, and towering *Argentinosaurus*.

Picassosaur

When Is a Rock Like J.K. Rowling?

Stones may be silent, but some can tell tales so long they make the Harry Potter series look short.

Millions of years ago, particles and mud settled on the bottom of lakes and oceans, piling muck upon muck and gradually hardening into rock. Clues trapped in the stone—including fossil remains of tiny animals or traces of chemicals—help scientists "read" what the air and climate were like long ago.

In China, researchers have drilled a thin core of rock so long it would take more than an hour to walk from end to end. Each layer in the core reveals climate information—and suggests that when dinosaurs ruled the planet between 65 and 145 million years ago, the air had 2 to 6 times more carbon dioxide than today. The gas heated the planet enough to make the surface of the Atlantic Ocean as steaming as a hot tub.

Rocks aren't the only prehistoric climate diaries. In such places as Greenland and Antarctica, chemicals held or trapped by layers of ice in ancient glaciers record climate history just like some rocks.

Darn it!

HOT ENOUGH?

The hottest temperature ever recorded was in Al 'Aziziyah, Libya (57.8° Celsius or 136° Fahrenheit), followed by a scorcher at Greenland Ranch in Death Valley, California (56.7° Celsius or 134° Fahrenheit).

11

Earth's Temperature Control Knob

Carbon dioxide—the stuff we produce when we burn things—is the world's most important temperature control knob, say scientists.

Throughout Earth's 4.5-billion-year history, water vapor in the sky has held the most heat but the most *change* in temperature has come from just a little more or less carbon dioxide. During the past half a million years, the amount of carbon dioxide has been less than 3 cups in every 10,000 cups of air. Yet a difference of a single cup—from almost 3 to less than 2—contributed to worldwide chills that sent ice-age glaciers marching into Europe and North America.

Adding a cup, on the other hand, helped warm the place up. About 15 million years ago, the amount of carbon dioxide was closer to 4 cups per 10,000 cups of air. The world was too toasty for big ice caps at the North and South Poles. Less ice on land meant more water in the oceans and higher sea levels. If you could travel back in time, you'd need scuba gear to visit today's favorite beaches. They would have been underwater to the depth of a 10-story building.

It's just not the same.

A FOOTPRINT bigger than a school desktop is startling to see anywhere, but in 1960 scientists Albert de Lapparent and Robert Laffitte were astonished when they spotted several gigantic three-toed steps embedded in rock on an island halfway between the tip of northern Europe and the frozen North Pole. The fossil prints belonged to a dinosaur that lived 100 million years ago, and their discovery surprised dinosaur researchers everywhere.

Most of us think these scaly monsters lived in the same places where modern reptiles are comfortable—in warm, mainly tropical areas. But the Arctic footprints, and other fossils found in northern Europe, Australia, Alaska, and even Antarctica, suggest many species of dinosaurs roamed the regions near the Earth's now icy poles.

Polar temperatures are generally believed to have been far less frigid then. Yet, even with the poles warmer than they are today, polar dinosaurs still had to survive the cold, dark winter months. A few probably visited only during the summer, migrating like birds to avoid the worst seasons. But some researchers wonder if polar dinosaurs generated their own heat the way humans and other warm-blooded animals do. Recent discoveries of large, fossilized tunnels in Australia suggest there were dinosaurs that took shelter, had babies, and lived in burrows they dug into the ground deep below the frozen surface.

Wear your scarf or you'll become extinct!

Hot Plates and Cold Plates

Antarctica, the ice-covered continent at the South Pole, is the coldest, harshest, iciest place on Earth. But would you believe that forest creatures once roamed its lush, green woods?

Sometime around 34 million years ago, the climate of Antarctica changed from fabulous to frigid, and scientists believe plate tectonics was the reason. Plate tectonics is the way landmasses such as continents constantly move, as they float like the broken pieces of a hard shell ("plates") over the globe's soft, molten inside. Sometimes all the pieces have even pressed together to form one supercontinent.

Antarctica used to be closely connected to South America and Australia. But by 50 to 20 million years ago, all three continents had completely drifted apart. A new sea passage allowed an ocean current to freely circle Antarctica, cutting it off from warmer seas. Isolated by this new chilling current, Antarctica slowly became the barren, icy land it is today.

PACK A LUNCH 250 million years ago, you could have hiked from British Columbia to Borneo without getting your feet wet.

BORNEO

BRITISH COLUMBIA

QUESTION 6
How big was the wallop that KO'd T. rex?

THIRTY YEARS AGO, when scientists Walter Alvarez and his dad, Luis, first suggested that a huge meteor—bigger than Manhattan Island—flattened the monstrous *Tyrannosaurus rex* and killed off the rest of the dinosaurs, many people thought they were crazy. The idea seemed like something out of a comic book.

Scientists now know better. Researchers found a vast crater in Mexico created by an asteroid so big it would have taken over two hours to walk across. The huge space boulder hit the Earth at about the time of the dinosaurs' demise 65 million years ago. The blast would have sent enough dust into the sky to block out the sun for years or even decades, causing a killer chill that finished off the dinosaurs and dramatically altered life on the planet.

You could call that bad luck for the dinosaurs, but many scientists believe the same fluky chance gave big dinosaurs a leg up in the first place. Evidence suggests the Earth may have been hit by another large meteor about 135 million years earlier that wiped out early reptiles and mammal ancestors, eliminating the competition.

uh oh!

When Dinosaurs ROCKED

300–250 million years ago
Life on Earth is evolving along merrily as early ancestors of reptiles and mammals thrive in friendly climates.

250 million years ago
Boom! History's deadliest mystery wipes out four of every five species. A volcanic inferno is likely to blame, but some science sleuths suspect a huge space rock colliding with Earth may have had a role.

200 million years ago
Boom: The Sequel! Another deadly extinction—possibly caused by another asteroid—knocks life on earth for a loop again.

200–65 million years ago
Life is back on track—and it's the fast track for dinosaurs. They step up to fill the gap left by creatures clobbered in the calamities, and begin to rule the world.

65 million years ago
Boom: The Finale! A massive meteor hits the Earth, but this time it's bad news for dinosaurs. Really bad. Dust and smoke fill the sky, chilling the whole planet. The mighty dinosaurs are wiped out forever.

IF A CASE OF PLANETARY GAS got things started on Earth, then it's not too surprising that a colossal belch a few billion years later helped propel mammals—the hairy, warm-blooded group to which we belong—to the head of the pack.

After the dinosaurs were clobbered into extinction, small mammals, once cowering in the shadows of scaly, meat-munching monsters, began to evolve into species of all shapes and sizes. But mammal evolution didn't really get cooking until the heat got turned up again after what scientists describe as a humungous "methane burp."

Many researchers believe that methane—a gas made of carbon and hydrogen that forms when dead things rot—collected in large pockets under the ocean floor, where the bodies of tiny creatures and plants had settled in deep layers. The theory suggests these methane storehouses abruptly opened about 55 million years ago, when a combination of warmer water and undersea landslides sent tremendous clouds of the stuff bubbling skyward.

Methane is one of the greenhouse gases that cause world temperatures to climb. It also reacts with oxygen to change into its chemical cousin, carbon dioxide. After the burp, global warming kicked in and lasted for about 170,000 years. The rapid changes created evolutionary opportunities for prehistoric mammals to evolve from the small creatures of dinosaur times to the ancestors of horses, tigers, deer, apes—and us.

DISCO PLANET
About one-third of the sun's light that hits Earth bounces back into space. Clouds and vapors, as well as snow and ice on the ground, reflect sunlight like the mirror ball at a disco.

QUESTION 8
Was this before
super-size fries and
jumbo meals?

THE DINO-DISAPPEARANCE was a big chance for mammals—
a really big chance.

While they shared the planet with dinosaurs for their first 140
million years, mammals were all little—the largest was no bigger
than a dog. After the dinosaur extinction and climate helped fire the
evolutionary change factory, mammals quickly evolved into species
more than a thousand times the size they had ever reached before.
The mega mammals had arrived.

The biggest mammal ever to roam the planet was a hornless
rhinoceros that weighed more than twice as much as the largest
elephant and was tall enough to peer through a second-story window
(if houses had existed at the time). *Indricotherium transouralicum*
(**inn**-drih-koe-**theer**-ee-um trans-oor-**ell**-ih-kum), as the beast is
known, chomped leaves and plants across Europe and Asia.

The mega mammals
lived about 34 million
years ago, taking
advantage of what
scientists believe
was a cooling climate,
because their larger
bodies were better at
keeping in heat.

They call me Mr. Big.

Clim-ACTivity:
BOTTLED UP

Some gases, such as oxygen, let the sun's energy pass right through them. Others, such as carbon dioxide, trap the heat. See for yourself.

You're hot! I know.

You need:
* a desk lamp with a regular incandescent bulb (not energy-saving or fluorescent)
* 2 jam jars with lids
* some vinegar
* ½ teaspoon baking soda
* 2 thermometers small enough to fit inside the jars

Heat Test:
1. Pour vinegar into each jar until it is as deep as your little finger is wide.
2. Place a thermometer in each jar, screw the lids on, and place the jars close to the bulb for about 5 minutes.
3. Write down the temperature of each jar, and let them cool away from the lamp for 10 minutes.
4. Next, add the baking soda to one of the jam jars and quickly close the lid.
5. Place both jars under the lamp for 5 minutes. What is the temperature in each jar now? What do you think happened?

ANSWER

Baking soda contains carbon and oxygen, and adding it to vinegar causes a chemical reaction that produces carbon dioxide. An incandescent bulb gives off infrared heat, like the sun, and the jar with carbon dioxide will absorb the heat and warm up more than the other jar.

CHAPTER 2

A HUMAN for ALL SEASONS

Good, now only two of my feet are freezing.

IF EVOLUTION IS A TRAIN, climate has often been the tracks. When climate shifted its path, creatures had to change direction too, evolving to cope with new surroundings.

The evolution of humans is no different. Our earliest ancestors—the hairy ape-like creatures that split from the chimpanzee group 5 to 8 million years ago—had to deal with changes ahead of the last ice age, which began about 2 million years ago. The world was getting colder, drier, and less predictable. These challenges may actually have helped us to become the all-season species we are today. Scientists argue that surviving tough weather may help explain why humans walk on two feet, how we became so smart, why we can run long distances, and even why we're the only human species left standing.

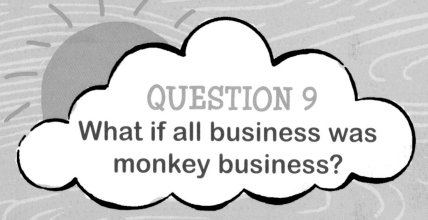

QUESTION 9
What if all business was monkey business?

THERE REALLY WAS A PLANET OF THE APES . . . and we're living on it.

It's true: between 22 million and 5.5 million years ago, apes ruled the roost across a large part of the world—from what's now France all the way to China and south to southern Africa. Although just a handful of ape species are alive today, back then as many as 100 different kinds of apes thrived in the forests and jungles of three continents, hanging about and going ape with not a zookeeper in sight. Scientists say the many ape varieties show the creative work of evolution: new apes evolved as they moved out of Africa and adapted to new environments in Europe and Asia. Several were great apes that shared similarities with the gorillas, chimpanzees, and orangutans of today.

Climate put an end to much of the monkey business, say researchers. As the gradual jostling of the planet's moving landmasses pushed the Himalayan Mountains and European Alps ever higher, the mountains became wind- and weather-warping features of the landscape. Ocean currents also changed, and a planetary cooling cycle formed ice caps at the poles. The climate overhaul turned Europe and Asia abruptly colder and large parts of Africa became dry. For many ape species, the change was too much.

Between 6 million and 5 million years ago, scores of European and Asian apes went extinct. Only two great ape lineages from these northern areas survived, and they did it, say researchers, by retreating south. One group moved to the warm jungles of southeast Asia, where it eventually gave rise to orangutans. And the other traveled to tropical Africa, where it put down the roots of our own human family tree.

ARDI IS ONE OF THOSE PEOPLE who always seem to stir up arguments.

Ardi is the nickname for a fossil skeleton of an early human-like ancestor. His scientific name is *Ardipithecus ramidus* (ar-dih-**pith**-eh-kuss **ram**-ih-duss) and he has researchers in a quarrel. They're bickering about whether our forebears walked using their knuckles, as modern apes and chimps do, or whether they stood tall and began strolling around almost as soon as they moved out of the woods.

Climate, agree scientists, likely had a lot to do with whatever mode of travel Ardi preferred. Ardi and the rest of his species lived in what's now Ethiopia, in northern Africa, about 4.4 million years ago. The Earth was cooling ahead of the last ice age, and Ardi's home was changing from dense forests to dry grasslands with few trees.

Ardi's hands and feet show he was clearly capable of getting around in trees. But he had also evolved the ability to walk upright, possibly without using his knuckles for support. If his hands were free, Ardi could carry fruit or a baby Ardi while crossing open ground. Walking would have helped him hunt, find food, and seek shelter as the drier climate created more space between trees, making it impossible to travel by swinging from branch to branch.

QUESTION 11
Is "food for thought" on the menu?

YOU ARE WHAT YOU EAT. Or at least your early ancestors were about 2.5 million years ago. That's when the world's cooling climate radically altered their menu. The result, say scientists, was a crossroads in human evolution that helps explain why people have such big brains.

The northern glaciers of the last ice age had begun to push deep into Europe, North America, and Asia. In Africa, home to several descendants of human-like apes called Australopiths, the climate got cooler, drier, and—most importantly—less predictable. Forests and familiar plants disappeared, and monkeys, tiny deer, and other woodland beasts were replaced by grassland animals such as antelope and wild pigs. Change was happening so fast, it was hard to know what to have for dinner.

Some apes, such as *Paranthropus* (puh-**ran**-thruh-pus), became specialist eaters, chomping up drier plants with bigger jaws. But a newly evolved group called *Homo erectus* made a different choice. Instead of continuing to munch the same fruits, nuts, and other foods they always had, these earliest humans went for the big buffet, developing skills to find new seeds and fruits, as well as hunting for birds' eggs and animals newly available in the changed landscape. This took a lot of brainpower, learning what foods were safe to eat, and when and where to find them in an unpredictable world. It paid off. *Paranthropus* disappeared about a million years ago, while the bigger-brained *Homo erectus* survived to give rise to new groups of early humans—including our own brainiac species, *Homo sapiens*.

The Australopith Restaurant Guide

CHEZ PARANTHROPUS   **HOMO ERECTUS
ALL-YOU-CAN-EAT BUFFET**

A Spinning Path to the Ice Ages

"Milly," said Mama Milanković as she watched her son play, "if you don't stop staring at those spinning tops, your eyes will start turning in your head."

Actually, no one knows if Milutin Milanković was fascinated by tops when he was a boy in central Europe over a century ago. But when he became a scientist, the twirling toys probably helped him picture the way the planet's movement affects climate.

The Earth spins in space around an imaginary line—or axis—through its middle. But it doesn't spin perfectly like a wheel around an axle; instead, it wobbles like a top. Milanković's calculations showed that roughly every 22,000 years, the Earth's wobble changes slightly. He also determined that the path our planet follows around the sun becomes less of a circle and more of an oval every 100,000 years or so.

It's not me, it's the planet!

Finally, Milanković figured out that the tilt of the Earth—the way its axis leans—also changes, tipping the top or bottom of the planet farther from the sun every 41,000 years.

Milanković's work helped explain why Earth's climate has alternated between warm when it's near the sun and, when it's distant, chilly enough to trigger ice ages.

GENIUS JANITOR
Decades before Milanković, James Croll of Scotland suggested a link between the Earth's orbit and ice ages. The self-trained scientist published his theory while working as a museum janitor in 1864.

All that for one penny an hour!

QUESTION 12
Is that why we're called the human race?

OLYMPIC COMPETITORS are impressive, but most of us would agree that the strength and agility of many animal athletes put weakling humans to shame. We've got the brains, but they have the brawn.

Not totally true, say scientists. Yes, we're smart, but we have other talents too. Running really far in hot weather is one of them. Humans, it turns out, can run farther and longer than many other animals known for their speed and power, including dogs, wolves, hyenas, and even cheetahs. All of those animals perspire by panting and can overheat if they run too far, too fast. Humans sweat through their skin, which helps them keep their cool. Athletes in top condition can jog quickly for hours at a time, some even covering ultra-marathon distances of 160 kilometers (100 miles) or more.

Endurance running is a gift that early humans probably owe to their altered surroundings in eastern Africa. Scientists suggest that our ancestors' ability to run likely evolved at the same time as their ability to walk upright. Running allowed hunters or scavengers to cover more ground in search of food, after a cooler climate transformed the African woodlands into open, grassy savanna.

QUESTION 13
Toba or not to be?

THAT IS THE QUESTION— or, at least, it was 71,000 years ago when humans may have nearly gone extinct after the eruption of Mount Toba in southeast Asia.

The Toba blast was the largest-known volcanic explosion in the past 2 million years, and thanks to the ash and chemicals it spewed into the air, little sunlight reached the Earth for years, causing a catastrophic climate change known as "volcanic winter." Scientists say Toba's eruption made even summers feel like living in a refrigerator. The worst of the volcanic winter lasted for six years, and the weather remained dry and cold for another thousand.

All life, including our own ancestors, struggled to carry on. Studies of human DNA suggest that many early people were wiped out by freezing temperatures and starvation. Neanderthals, our colder-climate cousins, may have fared better. But so few modern humans survived the dramatic event—eking out a precarious existence in a corner of Africa— that our entire species could have easily been pushed to extinction by another disaster or even by hungry bears, wild cats, and other predators.

Luckily for us, our handful of hardy ancestors clung to life and eventually repopulated the Earth.

Hotheads Keep Cool

Sometimes climate change is a blast—and not the fun kind. The thunderous eruptions of the world's volcanoes have a history of exploding our climate off course. In the far distant past, volcanoes shot carbon dioxide into the atmosphere and caused warming, but most volcanic gases reflect the sun's light and heat away from the Earth, cooling the air. A massive mountainous hothead can throw out so much ash and gas that it literally makes a dark cover over the world for weeks or months.

Chemical vapors called aerosols—mainly stinky, gaseous sulfur—can linger in the atmosphere even longer. Two centuries ago, an Indonesian volcano called Tambora exploded and sent more ash skyward than any other eruption in the past 500 years, and people half the world away were shivering a year later. In 1991, Mount Pinatubo erupted in the Philippines and temporarily halted the rise in sea levels caused by decades of global warming.

Even oceans can be cooled, far below the surface. Scientists say the deep sea can store the chilling effects of big volcanoes so that they last for decades or centuries.

QUESTION 14
Did we also beat them at video games?

WE HAVEN'T ALWAYS BEEN ALONE on the evolutionary ladder. Modern humans, *Homo sapiens*, appeared almost 200,000 years ago, and for most of our existence, we shared the planet with other kinds of humans. One was the rugged, heavy-browed Neanderthals, who thrived in Europe until as recently as 24,000 years ago.

So what happened that left us as the last humans standing? The mystery has fascinated scientists for decades, and many believe climate played a key role.

From about 118,000 until 15,000 years ago, the last ice age made life seriously chilled in northern Europe. As glaciers crept south, the Neanderthals living there were frozen out and moved south to escape the cold. At the same time, modern humans began moving out of Africa because the unstable climate was causing droughts and changing the plant and animal life. They hiked into Europe around 40,000 years ago as the Neanderthals were crowding south, until the two peoples lived side by side north of the Mediterranean Sea for 20,000 years or more.

Although Neanderthal DNA in Europeans today suggests that modern humans sometimes mated with their northern relatives, many scientists believe the two groups were fierce competitors. They hunted the same animals and lived in similar cave shelters. Modern humans, however, had the winning edge: technology. Researchers suspect *Homo sapiens* was the better hunter—and perhaps the better warrior, if the two groups battled—because their weapons and their tools, including bone fish hooks and needles to sew crude clothes, were superior to those of our doomed cousins.

QUESTION 15
Is this what they mean by "downsizing"?

GETTING THE MUNCHIES IS ONE THING, but did hungry humans really eat all the big animals of North America soon after arriving on the continent?

Megafauna is the word scientists use to describe the very large animals that once roamed many parts of the world, including what's now Canada and the United States. Mastodons, mammoths, giant sloths, and enormous saber-toothed cats all thrived in North America until about 11,000 years ago, when they quickly vanished.

What—or who—killed these big beasts remains a prehistoric whodunit mystery. Some scientists think the chief suspect is us. They argue that the megafauna became mega-meals after human hunters and their mega-appetites appeared. The same thing happened to all the large creatures after humans set foot in Australia (about 46,000 years ago), South America (about 15,000 years ago), and New Zealand (about 700 years ago).

Not so fast, say those who argue in our defense. In North
America, evidence points to another suspect—climate. The end
of the last major glaciation about 12,000 years ago meant the
continent was warming fast. The rapidly changing climate altered
the environment and made finding food tricky.

One thing is certain, though: mice were having the time of
their lives. As the North American ice sheets melted, and plants
and the land itself changed rapidly, animals large and small
struggled to live. As many as a third of mammal species in some
areas went extinct. Deer mice, however, not only survived, they
thrived. Fossils suggest these mice—which are not fussy eaters,
chomping seeds, berries, insects, or whatever else they find—
doubled their population, becoming the rulers of the forest by
sheer numbers.

URBAN ICING
Toronto and Chicago were really chillin' 20,000 years
ago. The land these cities stand on was buried under
ice up to 3 kilometers (2 miles) thick.

QUESTION 16
Did barn dances come later?

IF YOU LIKE TWANGIN' GUITARS, checked shirts, and overalls, maybe you should thank climate change . . . and the Natufians. Never heard of them? Well, they're not a country and western band, but the Natufians may have been the world's first farmers. Their name comes from Wadi al-Natuf, an area in modern Israel where evidence of these folk was discovered. Some scientists believe a global chill between 12,900 and 11,600 years ago, caused by an abrupt change in global ocean currents, inspired agriculture.

The Natufians hunted and gathered nuts, berries, and wild grains near the eastern end of the Mediterranean Sea. Unlike many early cultures, the Natufians set up permanent homes and even villages. The area's lush woodlands meant they didn't have to go far to find food.

Then the 1,300-year cold snap turned their homeland scrubby and dry. The foods the Natufians depended on struggled to survive, and so did the people. To ensure that they had enough to eat—so the theory goes—some of the people began to gather and plant grain seeds, tending and harvesting the crops. Farming was born, and human civilization (along with country music and clothes) was changed forever.

Ocean Motion Goes Cold

When an Arctic flower shows up all over Europe and North America, it may be time to check the heating system.

Many scientists believe the oceans are as important for heating the Earth as the sun is. Oceans store heat energy and move sun-warmed water along currents from the equator to the colder parts of the planet. Researchers say this heating system has sometimes broken down when the currents slowed or stopped altogether.

That's what appears to have happened about 12,900 years ago when Europe and North America experienced an abrupt big chill. The last ice age was ending, and the massive northern glaciers, melting in the warmer world, poured fresh water into the oceans. The frigid water interrupted the currents that deliver heat to the north.

A cold-loving Arctic flower called the white dryas found it could live almost anywhere. The climate stayed chilly for almost 13 centuries. Scientists call this cold spell the "Younger Dryas" after the flourishing flower.

Someone want a boiler fixed?

Clim-ACTivity:
THE EVOLUTION OF HUMOR SAPIENS

Q: What did the fossil cow say to the African anthropologist?

A: "I have some important moos for you."

Fossils that show evolutionary changes in the African ancestors of cows (the family that includes antelopes, cattle, and goats) are helping researchers piece together climate-related shifts in the landscape—such as forests becoming grasslands—that may have also influenced early human evolution.

Q: What do you call a bowl of dry sand served after dinner?

A: Sahara dessert.

Between 15,000 and 5,000 years ago, the Sahara Desert wasn't so deserted. Changes in our planetary orbit meant the tropical monsoon rains reached that region. Humans lived and hunted in Saharan forests before the monsoon shifted again into a barren land of sand dunes and an area nearly as large as the United States transformed into a barren land of sand dunes and rocky plains.

CHAPTER 3

GONE with the WIND

Have you canceled the mail?

ACME MOVERS

IF YOU CAN'T STAND THE HEAT—the old saying goes—get out of the kitchen. For humans, too much heat or too little, too much rain or not enough have often been good reasons to pack up and move. When what's brewing overhead has made hunting or growing food hard or impossible, or even changed the landscape, a new address was a good way to ensure we survived.

Sometimes climate changes didn't kick us out as much as they coaxed us out. A shift to a kinder and gentler sky has inspired humans to feats of exploration that opened frontiers in every corner of the globe.

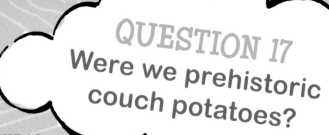

Were we prehistoric couch potatoes?

HUMANS ARE NATURAL-BORN LOAFERS—we only got going anywhere, say scientists, after climate gave us a push.

In the past 60,000 years, we humans have been busy adventurers. We've traveled, discovered, and settled in every corner of our now populated planet. But for the first 130,000 to 140,000 years of our existence, we barely budged from the African homeland where we first evolved. Although a group of modern humans may have journeyed as far as the Arabian peninsula 125,000 years ago, researchers have puzzled over the fact that most of us preferred prehistoric hanging around until, all at once, we got a move on. One explanation is climate change.

Beginning 70,000 to 80,000 years ago, ice-age glaciers were reaching south into Europe and North America. The climate of central Africa, where humans were happily hunting gazelles and gathering plants, was affected too. Research suggests the African rain came in downpours or, for long periods, not at all. Its unpredictability transformed the landscape that had been so agreeable to our early ancestors.

The weird weather appears to have finally unsettled our human forebears, who packed their kits and headed out of Africa to search for friendlier lands—loafers no more.

QUESTION 18
Didn't there use to be a bridge around here?

TIMING IS EVERYTHING WHEN YOU TRAVEL. Just ask the first people to arrive in North America: they had to schedule their trip to dodge some fast-closing roadblocks and cross a disappearing bridge to get here.

These hazards of their journey—more typical of a computer game adventure than a story of human migration—were courtesy of a changing climate, say scientists.

By the time modern humans reached the eastern edge of Asia 40,000 years ago or so, the last ice age had created massive ice sheets covering large parts of Europe, Asia, and North America. Scientists say these glaciers had locked enormous amounts of the Earth's water in ice, leaving sea levels lower than today's by about 90 meters (300 feet)—the height of the Statue of Liberty. The low levels created a bridge of dry land that reached across the modern-day Bering Strait from Siberia to North America.

Before the glaciers reached their peak size, a group of humans—possibly as few as 5,000 people—squeezed through an ice-free corridor between central Asia and Siberia. The ice then closed the gap for thousands of years. Isolated from the rest of Asia, many of these adventurers trooped across the land bridge, called Beringia, into what is now Alaska. As the glaciers receded, they began walking south and east sometime after 16,500 years ago, making their way into the rest of North and South America.

They had to move forward because there was no going back. Sea levels quickly rose again as the great glaciers melted. Ocean waters closed over Beringia and the Asia–North America link was lost under the waves.

Good grief, only half a million years until the land bridge closes!

Climate, Abridged

Sometimes climate works like a drawbridge-keeper. It can create land bridges, or make them disappear.

Land bridges have been important links between islands or continents, allowing plants and animals, including humans, to spread. These strips of dry land appear or disappear as sea levels rise and fall thanks to the warming and cooling of the earth. During ice ages, glaciers and ice sheets suck up water, and seas recede.

The Bering Strait land bridge—Beringia—is probably the best known. But scientists believe other land bridges from glacial times linked Britain and Europe, Sri Lanka and India, southeast Asia and the Indonesian islands, and New Guinea and Australia.

LONDON BRIDGES
During the last ice age, lower sea levels joined Britain to mainland Europe by a land bridge known as Doggerland. Rising water isolated the island around 6500 BC.

Shortcut to South America

The native people of North and South America can thank their Asian ancestors for finding a way across the Bering Strait to the New World. But as these ancient migrants made their way south, did they get the feeling that someone else had been there first?

Most scientists believe people from northern Asia moved deeper into the Americas as the warming climate melted the glaciers, allowing the travelers to reach the southwestern United States by 13,500 years ago. But stone tools and other evidence of people living in Monte Verde, Chile, nearly 2,000 years earlier have researchers scratching their heads. How could the migrating people possibly have moved so quickly the length of two continents, across a lot of terrain still gripped by ice?

The puzzle remains unsolved, but most researchers believe some early people bypassed glaciers by traveling along the coast. Others suggest that immigrants from southeastern Asia may have reached the Americas by sea even before the northerners arrived.

They will never know the truth.

Have you got the foggiest idea where we are?

CHRISTOPHER COLUMBUS must have had a good publicity agent. The 15th-century Italian sailor enjoyed credit for centuries as the first European to discover America. In many countries, the Columbus Day holiday still celebrates the event—even though Bjarni Herjolfsson beat Columbus to the punch by about 500 years.

More than 1,200 years ago, the world's climate abruptly warmed up, and it stayed that way for five centuries. Why it happened isn't clear. Some researchers believe the sun was more active, bombarding the Earth with more of its energy. Later named the Medieval Warm Period, this climate shift created ideal sailing conditions for restless explorers—especially the Vikings of the North Atlantic.

Not long after the warm period began, Viking sailors from Norway settled Iceland and, after that, Greenland. Bjarni was a Viking merchant, and his dad was among the Greenland colonists. In 985 or 986 CE, Bjarni decided to stop by for a visit. After sailing to Iceland, he set off with his crew for the two- or three-day trip to Greenland, but was blown off course. Bjarni was soon utterly lost in a thick fog, drifting with the wind and tides. Before eventually finding his way back, the puzzled Viking sailed for days along the shore of the then-unknown continent of North America.

Another adventurous Viking, Leif Eriksson, later heard Bjarni's story and retraced the first voyage. Leif is believed to be the first European to have stepped ashore in North America, landing somewhere along the coast of Labrador in Canada.

The Dotty Sun

Even the sun can get up on the wrong side of the bed. Sometimes it has energy to burn; other times, it doesn't have its usual spark.

According to scientists, the searing ball of gases glows with more or less oomph depending on the amount of electrically charged activity on its surface. Sunspots provide clues to the sun's get-up-and-go. These brightly bordered dark spots are caused by concentrations of churning magnetic energy, and many are bigger than Earth itself. A high number of sunspots signals a high level of energy being beamed to Earth and heating us up.

Italian astronomer Galileo Galilei first described sunspots in the 1600s, and since then scientists have noticed that the sun cycles from having hundreds of dots to showing few or almost no spots at all. These cycles happen about every 11 years, but the maximum number of spots in each cycle can also change. Sometimes, periods with few or many sunspots last for decades.

I can't go to the universe today, Mom.

QUESTION 20
Did they wear their lifejackets?

THE MEDIEVAL WARM PERIOD meant smooth sailing not just for the Vikings, but in many other parts of the planet too.

The Polynesian people of Fiji, Samoa, and Tonga, for example, reckoned the inviting weather signaled a good time to take their canoes out for a spin—a very long spin. Using slender, open boats with an outrigger pontoon for stability, or two canoes attached by poles, they crossed vast tracts of tossing ocean to reach dozens of remote islands throughout the South Pacific. Between about 800 and 1200 CE, these intrepid paddlers discovered and settled outposts as far flung as Hawaii, Easter Island (also called Rapa Nui), and, finally, a few centuries later, New Zealand. How far flung was that? Well, getting from Fiji, where some of the Polynesian adventurers may have started, to Easter Island would take more paddling power than canoeing from New York City to London, England.

Exploration and even trade between the Pacific island settlements came to an abrupt halt after the climate grew cooler and more turbulent again in the 14th century—the beginning of the Little Ice Age.

Let's go on a Pacific cruise you said!

47

QUESTION 21
Did you just blow into town?

"A blow for Spain!"

SIR FRANCIS DRAKE had some very influential friends. Sure, the 16th-century sailor was a slave trader and a pirate, but Queen Elizabeth I was a close pal. Drake's friends in high places even appear to have included another important ally—the climate.

Climate was important to explorers, but it was also crucial for sailing to wage war. In 1588, a flotilla of about 130 Spanish ships called the Great Armada sailed north up the European coast to attack England. Drake was second-in-command of the English Royal Navy, and he met the Armada with a fleet of almost the same number of British ships.

Drake was declared a hero after his daring attacks—including setting old British ships alight and sending them into the midst of the Armada—helped defeat the Spanish. But researchers say climate actually struck a more decisive blow. The battle took place in the middle of a 500-year cold snap known as the Little Ice Age.

Throughout much of the world, the climate grew chilly, wet, and tumultuous soon after the end of the Medieval Warm Period. Some researchers suggest it was caused by a long period of very few sunspots, when less energy was warming the Earth. Cool temperatures were accompanied by fierce storms.

After the battle, the Armada sailed north to round the tip of Scotland and then south in the wind-whipped Atlantic Ocean, trying to reach home. When the Spanish ships reached the open sea off Ireland, harrowing gales were waiting. The squalls shredded sails and toppled masts. With no way to steer, many of the helpless boats were smashed to pieces against the craggy Irish coast. Twenty-four ships were lost to the storm, more than were destroyed by Drake and his navy.

QUESTION 22
Why doesn't this place look like the postcards?

THE PICTURES SHOWED A SUNNY PARADISE, complete with pineapples, basking crocodiles, and cheerful natives. Who wouldn't leave dreary, damp England for a land of warmth and easy living?

In 1587, more than 100 Londoners did just that after they saw the bright paintings that John White had made during an expedition to North America a couple of years earlier. The eager migrants agreed to travel to the New World to start the first English colony, an effort meant to discourage Spain from acquiring too much influence there.

The settlers, led by White and including his pregnant daughter and her husband, crossed the ocean and landed on Roanoke Island off the shores of what is now North Carolina. They probably saw that it didn't look much like the pictures (there were no pineapples), but at least it was July and the weather was warm. In August, White's granddaughter was born, and White reluctantly sailed back to England for supplies. An English sea war with Spain prevented his return for almost three years. When he finally got back to Roanoke, the place was deserted—the colony had completely disappeared. White tried to search for them, but never found his family or any of the other settlers.

No one has ever solved the mystery of the Lost Colony, but scientists now believe climate had a hand in it. Researchers studied the growth rings of ancient trees to build a climate history of the eastern United States. The tree rings showed that the period between 1587 and 1589 marked the driest three-year stretch in 700 years. The drought was particularly severe in the area around Roanoke.

Many believe the colony members could not grow enough food and starved. Others suggest the settlers may have survived by joining a nearby Chesapeake native tribe.

New World "Unsettlements"

I'll keep your dinner warm dear.

1492
"Hey, there's a continent over there." Spaniard Chris Columbus takes a cruise, and Europe gets wind of North America.

1521
Spain takes an early lead in the race to create new colonies on the continent. Hernán Cortés begins "New Spain" in Mexico after finishing off the Aztecs. England looks on in envy.

July 1587
Sir Walter Raleigh sends John White and 100 other English men, women, and children to Roanoke Island, North Carolina, to start a colony there.

August 1587
"Er . . . I forgot something." White returns to England for supplies and gets stuck there by a sea war with Spain.

1590
Poof! The entire colony has disappeared. White finally returns to Roanoke to find the place deserted. None of the settlers are ever seen again.

Can you ever be too far ahead of your time?

WHEN BRITISH EXPLORER
Sir John Franklin set sail from London on May 19, 1845, his plan made perfect sense: sailing across the top of the world would be a far faster route to Asia than rounding South America or navigating the Indian Ocean. He believed he could find a water route, named the Northwest Passage, through the islands of the Arctic Ocean. Everyone was so confident, the wives and girlfriends of the crew posted their letters to China.

Months later, somewhere in the frigid Canadian Arctic, Franklin, along with 128 other men aboard the ships *Erebus* and *Terror*, vanished. After a decade of searching, a few graves and some equipment were uncovered on an Arctic island. Also found were notes suggesting the ships had become hopelessly trapped in ice. But details of the expedition's disappearance remained a mystery and a warning—seeking a Northwest Passage was a dangerous fantasy.

The route may have been impossible then, but today's changing climate is heating up Franklin's dream. The Arctic, say scientists, is warming almost twice as fast as other parts of the world, and its sea ice is melting. Many predict the Northwest Passage will be ice-free in the summer by 2030 and regularly open to boat traffic even earlier. This would cut about two weeks of sailing time, or more than a quarter of the distance, from the usual shipping route from Europe to Asia through the Panama Canal.

ok now, everybody push!

Clim-ACTivity:

PATHS OF THE PAST

Since the arrival of people in South America some 15,000
years ago, modern humans have settled on almost every
major landmass on the planet. But how we got there is
not entirely clear.

Most people believe modern humans evolved in eastern
Africa about 200,000 years ago and began our march out
of that continent about 60,000 years ago. Sometimes
climate shifts removed glacial roadblocks or created land
bridges to help—or stall—us along the way.

Can you connect the dots of the earliest known arrival dates of humans to guess how humans traveled from Africa to populate the world? See page 107 for solution.

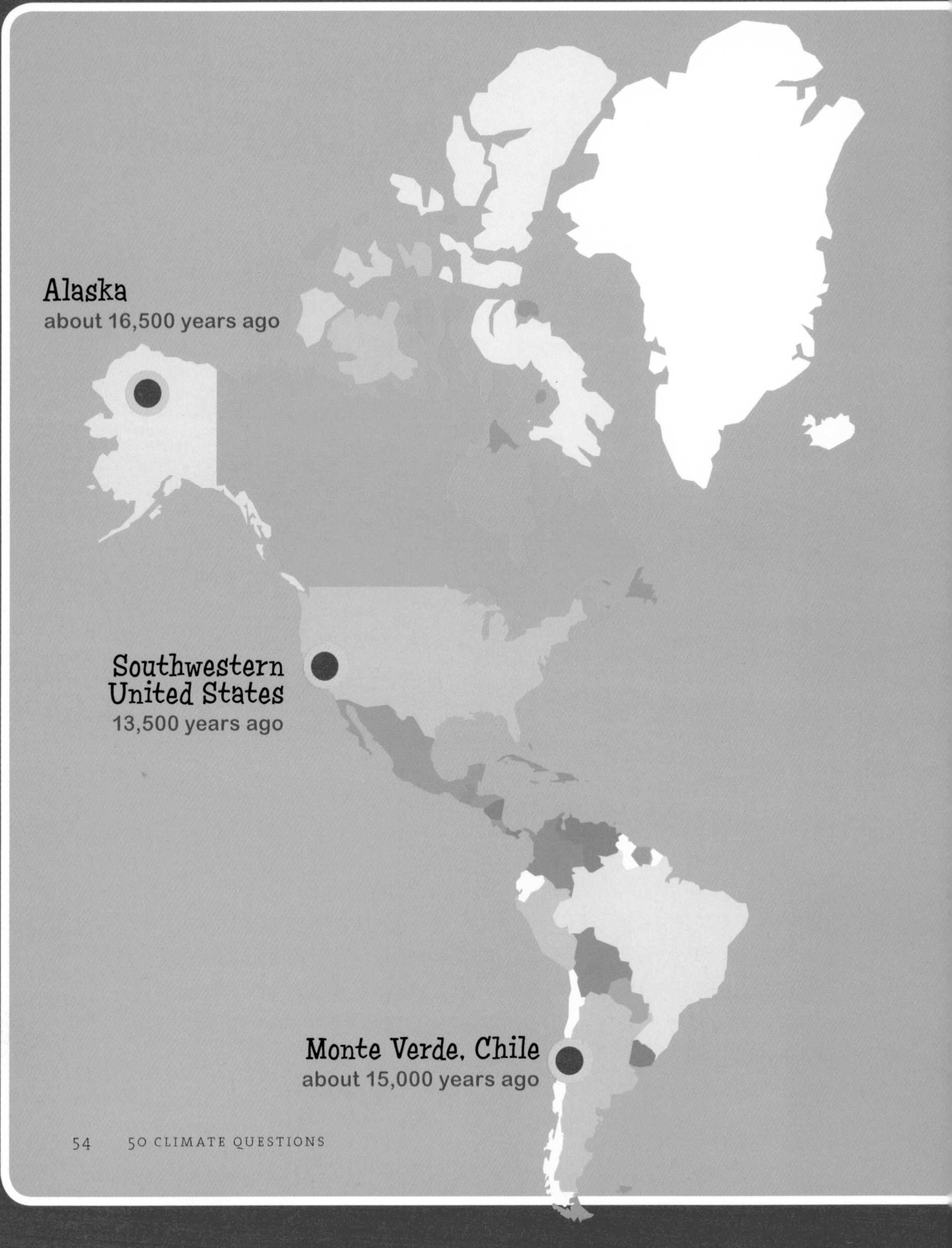

Alaska
about 16,500 years ago

Southwestern
United States
13,500 years ago

Monte Verde, Chile
about 15,000 years ago

Siberia
40,000 years ago

Europe
40,000 years ago

Hawaii
about 1,000
years ago

Fiji
3,000
years
ago

East Africa
200,000 years ago

Australia
50,000–40,000 years ago

New Zealand
750 years ago

CHAPTER 4

WHEN the SKY GODS ARE ANGRY

Where's my coffee?

HORUS IS THE GREATEST, said the Egyptians. Jupiter rules, said the Romans. Give me Dyaus any day, said the ancient Hindus. All over the world, as far back as anyone can remember, human civilizations worshipped their own version of a sky god. That's because early people everywhere knew that nothing was more important than good, dependable weather. It meant a rich harvest and reliable water. If their sky god didn't deliver, people would starve.

Throughout human history, natural climate upheavals have played the role of a moody sky god—helping ancient societies grow and prosper, and sometimes, without warning, bringing terrible destruction to entire civilizations.

KING NARAM-SIN was royally ticked off. Two of his fortune-tellers had told him his luck was going to turn bad, and he didn't like what he heard. This occurred about 4,200 years ago, long before even the ancient Greeks or Romans were around.

Naram-sin was emperor of the kingdom of Akkad, the world's first empire. It was created by Naram-sin's grandfather, Sargon, after he conquered the lands known as Mesopotamia in and around modern-day Iraq. Naram-sin blamed the soothsayers themselves for the rotten news and decided to vent his frustration by ordering an attack on their temple—a monument built to honor the sky god called Enlil. It was a bad idea. According to researchers, Akkad was soon hit by a terrible drought and fierce winds. The dry period lasted for 300 years, and the kingdom's crops withered. People fled or died, and whole cities were swallowed by drifting sand. The empire was destroyed.

Today, we know that the Akkadian collapse was not the work of an angry sky god. Possible causes are sunspot cycles, a change in ocean currents, or a change in the belt of air that circles the Earth near the equator, called the intertropical convergence zone, but no definite reason for the dry spell has been found yet. Scientists do know that the climate catastrophe that wiped out Akkad was so powerful it was felt as far away as Europe and even South America.

TABLET TALES
Archeologists found the story of the collapse of Akkad carved into clay tablets buried in sand. "The Curse of Akkad" was written less than a century after the disaster.

I think I'll wait for the movie.

The Curse of Akkad

Listen people, it will rain soon... sometime... er... I hope... please, Horus?

QUESTION 25
May I have a glass of water, mummy?

MODERN SCIENTISTS are often amazed by the clever ways the ancient Egyptians preserved dead bodies. Some of these mummies—carefully dried and wrapped in linen—are still around after more than 5,000 years. Equally impressive are pyramids as high as 45-story apartments, built without modern machinery, using stone blocks the size of cars. Obviously, the Egyptians were no dummies.

Even so, say researchers, their smarts were put to the test when the Nile River dried up. Scientists believe the same three-century drought that destroyed the Akkadian empire 4,200 years ago also dramatically shrank Egypt's main waterway. The vital farmlands on the Nile River delta became parched fields of cracked mud. People began to starve and to fight among themselves.

For the ruling pharaohs, it was bad news. For centuries, pharaohs had held power by claiming they were gods themselves. When the grain ran out, the jig was up. People realized their kings weren't really best buddies with the sky god Horus and had no influence over the rain or the climate. Egypt fell into a period of chaos and war known as the Egyptian Dark Ages.

After a few decades, Egyptian towns began to develop irrigation systems to help grow crops, and the civilization got back on its feet. But the days of the all-powerful pharaohs were gone for good.

Have You Seen My Civilization? I Think It's Lost.

Sometimes the sky gods must be in cahoots. The Akkadian Empire was toppled at the same time the famous kingdom of Egypt fell. But another bit of sky god handiwork is far less well known. When the ancient Harappan civilization collapsed, it left little more than a question mark.

Although Harappan towns flourished in the Indus Valley, in what is now Pakistan, at about the same time ancient Egypt was thriving, they vanished almost without a trace. The "lost civilization" of the Harappans had its own writing system and used the world's first oven-fired bricks. It also relied on the Indus River for water to grow food.

But, like Egypt, the Harappan world failed around 2200 BCE, probably destroyed by the same crop-killing drought. Unlike Egypt, Harappan society ended, and little was known of it until less than 100 years ago. Gold, jewelry, pots, and the remains of buildings were finally uncovered where a rich culture had all but disappeared from history.

Somewhere in Ancient Egypt

Meanwhile, in Akkad (roughly modern-day Iraq)

Meanwhile, in the Harappan Civilization (in modern-day Pakistan)

What did it look like?

Lost and Found Civilizations

When did you last see it?

Lost and Found Civilizations

Was it insured?

Lost and Found Civilizations

59

QUESTION 26
Did they bring their
own deck chairs?

We're not coming.

WHEN NOAH CALLED OUT his last "All aboard!" and kicked the giant gangplank from his ark full of animals, he knew the god of *his* sky was angry. The Lord had warned him that the world was a mess and needed a thorough washing. Noah probably wasn't thinking about climate change when the rains began. These days, however, some scientists believe the Bible story of Noah's flood may be based on true events from an ancient episode of global warming.

About 15,000 years ago, nearing the end of the last ice age, the huge glaciers covering Europe and North America began to melt. Water from the shrinking ice poured into the world's seas and oceans. The Mediterranean Sea filled up like a bathtub. About 7,500 years ago, it spilled over the brim at the eastern end, where the country of Turkey is now, and flooded a low area we call the Black Sea.

Unfortunately, early farmers had built villages there. Researchers say sea water gushed into the basin with the force of 200 Niagara Falls, drowning the lakeside land. Whole villages were submerged. Those who escaped spread the tale of the great flood.

QUESTION 27
Is it time to rethink your choice of gift?

THE ANCIENT MAYANS got a lot of things right. Nearly 2,000 years ago, they carved a civilization out of the dense forests of Central America. For 900 years, they built large, busy cities and developed a sophisticated culture that included written language, astronomy, art, and architecture . . . Oh, and they also held big parties for their gods where they sliced people open, reached under their ribs, and violently yanked out their still-beating hearts.

Sure, the Mayans didn't sacrifice humans as often as some other ancient cultures in the Americas, but they believed ritual killing was a good way to show a god they cared—especially their rain god, Chaac. Rain was vital to maize, the original corn, and maize was vital to feed the people. Keep Chaac happy, they reasoned, and everybody's happy.

It didn't quite work out. Some researchers believe the end of the Mayan civilization was triggered by a shift in the inter-tropical convergence zone circling the Earth near the equator. This belt of air is where winds from the northern and southern tropics meet, bringing clouds and rain.

The Mayans were used to this belt moving south for the winter, leaving their homeland dry for months. They counted on its return each summer to bring rain for their crops. But one summer the belt stayed farther south—and for the next several summers too. Water ran out, and so did food. All their grisly sacrifices couldn't save Mayan society from falling apart.

Three monster droughts, each lasting from years to decades, hit the region between 760 and 910 CE. Wars erupted between those with supplies and those without. The cities were abandoned, and the last of the Mayans faded into the countryside in search of water.

oh! you shouldn't have.

WASHOUT
In the late sixth century, torrential rains swept down the mountains of northern Peru and washed most of the Moche people's major city into the sea.

QUESTION 28
Et tu,
Climate?

Visigoth?
Honey did you
order a
Visigoth?

OF ALL THE ROMAN GODS, Jupiter had the worst temper. He also liked to meddle in human affairs. Maybe that's why the Roman Empire—among the largest, wealthiest, and most sophisticated nations in history—was the stage for some of the greatest dramas. A dying Julius Caesar whispered "Et tu, Brute?" (Latin for "You too, Brutus?") to the former friend who helped to murder him. Brilliant Roman military leader Mark Antony fell for Egypt's Queen Cleopatra. Emperor Nero famously fiddled while Rome burned.

The fall of Rome is among those well-known tales. The beginning of the end, after 800 years of uninterrupted dominion in large parts of Europe and North Africa, is often considered to be 410 CE. That's when, one late-summer night, a group of slaves secretly opened a gate in the city wall, and the Visigoth army from the east poured in to conquer the imperial city.

Recent research, however, suggests that the slaves and Visigoths were not alone in finally toppling the empire—climate was there too. Scientists looked at ancient growth rings in wood from European medieval castles and Roman ruins to discover a history of climate change. Wide growth rings match years with good growing conditions, while thin rings correspond to years of extreme dry or cold.

The rings revealed that the years between 250 and 550 CE—the same time the Roman Empire collapsed—were a period of climate upheaval. The weather from season to season went from wet to dry and warm to cold, and the poor crops could not feed the citizens. Weakened by famine and starvation, Romans could no longer defend themselves from enemies.

HIGH AND DRY
The driest place on Earth is thought to be Atacama Desert in Chile. Parts of this plateau have not felt rain since humans began keeping track over 400 years ago.

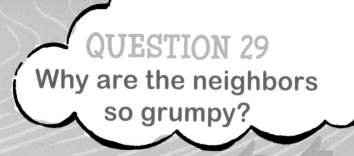

PEOPLE OF THE TIWANAKU CIVILIZATION dwelled so high up in the Andean Mountains of South America, they lived practically next door to their sky gods. That's how they found out that neighbors aren't always neighborly.

Tiwanaku society was a sprawling South American empire that flourished for more than a thousand years beside the highest lake in the world, Lake Titicaca. The capital city, Tiwanaku, stood on the lake's shores at about 3,800 meters (12,500 feet) above sea level.

The civilization began in about 300 BCE as a community of farmers who knew the tricks of growing food in the mountains— terraced fields and irrigation ditches. Soon their villages grew into cities. Tiwanaku builders used enormous sandstone blocks to construct palaces and monuments to their gods of the sun and weather. Before long, the empire and its ruling elites controlled towns and trade all the way to the Pacific Ocean.

A lasting shift in the mountain climate changed their world, say researchers. Beginning in about 1100 CE, the usual summer rains failed to come— year after year. The water level of Lake Titicaca fell by enough to leave a completely submerged five-story building high and dry. The sky gods had turned off the neighborhood tap. As crops failed, so did the Tiwanaku civilization.

Hey! Keep the noise down will ya!

Great, I fall for a guy who lives in a swamp!

QUESTION 30
Should we call her *Mer*maid Marian?

OUR SHIFTING CLIMATE has shaped beliefs and superstitions through the ages, and also helped spin a tale or two. Robin Hood, for one, is a centuries-old legend that had its start during the Medieval Warm Period. Robin Hood's story—of an outlaw hero who defied an evil king and lived in the forest with Maid Marian and his Merry Men—is thought to be based on the real-life exploits of a daring English rebel called Hereward the Wake. Hereward led a band of men near the Isle of Ely and battled the soldiers of King William the Conqueror after the Norman ruler invaded England in 1066.

Ely is now a coastal city about a two-hour drive north of London. But during the Medieval Warm Period, between 800 and 1300 CE, Ely was an island surrounded by marshes. Warmer global temperatures raised sea levels around the world as glaciers and ice sheets melted. Ely's countryside flooded, creating channels, marshes, and forested islets. Hereward and his band knew every inch of this tricky terrain, making it a perfect marshy hideout.

Robin Hood's story lives on, but no one knows what became of Hereward. News of his fate appears to have vanished along with the swamps around Ely.

You'll Love This House, God

Don't call us ungrateful. When Europe's climate became nice and stayed that way for almost 500 years during the Medieval Warm Period, Christians across the continent thanked God for it—by building ever more spectacular churches for Him.

The classic Gothic-style Notre Dame cathedral in Paris was one example. It took about 200 years to complete after work began in 1159. The awe-inspiring Notre-Dame de Chartres cathedral in northern France was completed in 1195. In England, the massive Canterbury Cathedral was constructed beginning in 1070, after the original was destroyed by fire. Another famous English church, the Lincoln Cathedral, was also built during this time. After its central bell tower was raised in 1311, the cathedral boasted almost 250 years as the tallest building in the world—higher than the Great Pyramid of Giza in Egypt, which had held the record for the previous 4,000 years.

IT'S NO ACCIDENT that the tradition of Halloween, with its
ghosts and witches, got its start in the 16th century. That's when
the popularity of magic and superstition reigned over common
sense. It was a time when some people believed saying the names
of the three biblical wise men could cure a person of epilepsy. It
was also—tragically—a time when many believed that broom-
riding witches were a real thing.

At least 40,000 people were burned to death, strangled,
beheaded, or otherwise killed in Europe between 1550 and 1650
because their neighbors and churches accused them of witchcraft.
In the Lorraine region of France, 2,700 convicted witches were
killed in a period of less than 40 years.

While superstition was the culprit, researchers now believe
climate may have played a part. The witch hunts happened during
the Little Ice Age, a period of cold and unpredictable weather
between about 1400 and 1900. Temperatures were often unusually
frigid, with crop-killing frosts, storms, and crazy weather that
caused many to imagine that witches must be at work.

Clim-ACTivity:
ANCIENT ANASAZI MYSTERY

More than a thousand years ago, the Anasazi people—ancestors of the Navajos—built a thriving civilization in the stark landscape of Chaco Canyon, New Mexico. They hunted, grew corn, beans, and squash, and created beautiful pottery containers and figures. Their massive apartment-like buildings, called pueblos, were built right into the cliff walls, and could house several thousand people. Then, sometime between 800 and 900 years ago, the Anasazi abruptly vanished. But why?

The clue: Scientists studied the growth rings from ancient trees around the area—including wood from pueblo beams. About 900 years ago, the tree rings began to be very close together for long periods of time. What do you think happened?

ANSWER

Close rings suggest tree growth was stunted. The region appears to have been wracked by terrible droughts that drove the Anasazi out of their amazing canyon home.

Does anyone see a rain cloud out there?

CHAPTER 5

WAR, PLAGUE, and the SCOOP on POOP

IF YOU THINK NATURAL CLIMATE UPHEAVALS are ancient history, think again. Climate has been messing with human plans right up to the present day. The long warm spell that opened the way for North America's first explorers happened a few centuries ago, but volcanoes and El Niños are recent news.

Historians like to talk about the people who have shaped civilizations—leaders such as Julius Caesar, Genghis Khan, and Napoleon Bonaparte—but climate has often played a role in events too. And unlike other famous players, climate is still very much on stage.

QUESTION 32
How does a
"golden age" lose
its polish?

A POEM CALLED "Many people come to visit and bring wine after I fell off my horse, drunk" may not sound like it belongs to a highly respected collection of verse, but it does. It was written by a famous poet named Du Fu who lived more than 1,200 years ago during China's Tang dynasty, a period many believe was among the most significant in early Chinese art and culture—that is, until the climate changed.

The Tang dynasty (618–907) was a time when China was ruled by the same royal family for three peaceful centuries. Painting, sculpture, and literature flourished. Even government officials were expected to be poets.

So why did this Chinese "golden age" come to a screeching halt? Recently, researchers discovered clues in two metals, iron and titanium, buried in layers of lake-bottom mud in southeastern China. Iron shows chemical differences after being exposed to oxygen from the air, called oxidation. A high amount of oxidized iron in a mud layer means the lake was being tossed and stirred by heavy winds. The titanium settled as wind-blown dust, and larger amounts also revealed especially gusty periods. Meanwhile, cave stalagmites formed by dripping water showed how much rain had fallen. The scientists found years of winter gales and weak summer rains that matched the timing of the Tang dynasty collapse. Crops withered on the parched land, followed by widespread famine that likely helped spark the fierce rebellion that brought down the last Tang ruler.

BIG DRIP

Stalagmites are climate history sticks. Made by dripping water so saturated with minerals that it condenses into stone "icicles," stalagmites reveal how much rain has fallen in years past by their rate of growth.

Been waiting long?

A simple funeral would have been better.

QUESTION 33
What's the weirdest weapon ever?

IMAGINE YOU'RE AN Italian soldier in the town of Caffa on the Black Sea. The year is 1345, and you're feeling good. The Mongol warriors who have been attacking your walled city for the past two years are losing strength. For some reason, great numbers of them are dying.

One day, you see a strange shape in the sky, and *wham!* a dead body lands at your feet with a sickening thud. *Wham, wham!* More come raining down—the Mongols are catapulting their dead into the town.

Many believe the Mongols at Caffa were the first army to use "weapons of mass destruction," a term used today for nuclear bombs and poisonous gases. That's because the missile-Mongols had died from bubonic plague, a deadly infectious disease that spread rapidly across Asia. The catapulted cadavers infected soldiers and also sailors, who then carried the contagion home to Europe. There, one out of every three people—as many as 50 million Europeans—died from the disease.

Climate, say researchers, had a hand in this biological warfare. Years earlier, the world's weather scene had shifted. China was inundated with driving rain and floods. The unusual wet and cold drowned or froze millions of rats, driving plague-carrying fleas from their preferred ratty hosts onto humans. When infected fleas bit a person, the plague bacteria entered the body and multiplied, and could cause death within days.

Seasonal Players

Many life-altering climate changes are heavy hitters. They're caused by monumental natural events that happen over many years—sometimes over centuries or even millennia. Shifts in our planet's orbit around the sun, sunspot cycles, and the seesaw of carbon dioxide levels all usually take their time, and their impacts have been long-lasting too.

Some climate changes are more like minor league players. These shifts last long enough to be considered more than simply a change in the weather, but they're counted in weeks or months. El Niño and La Niña climate events are like that. These can reach around the world after they are triggered over the Pacific Ocean, but seldom last longer than a year and a half. Many volcanoes affect world temperatures for short periods too. The gases and ash that explode into the air after big eruptions usually disappear within a few seasons.

Your turn.

EL NIÑO

LA NIÑA

EL NIÑO is a Spanish phrase meaning "the little boy." It's also the name for the Earth's shortest natural climate upheaval. Short doesn't mean puny or unimportant, because this kid packs a punch: El Niño climate events are well-known for knocking worldwide weather patterns for a loop.

YIPPEE!

An El Niño regularly appears every two to seven years, and each time, its strength and reach are hard to predict. The events always begin in the tropical Pacific—triggered by a particular mix of weak winds and warm water that affect air and weather patterns—but they can set off a domino effect around the planet.

The worst El Niño on record lasted from 1789 to 1793 and caused deadly droughts from Africa and India all the way to Indonesia and Australia, as well as weather extremes in Europe.

La Niña—"the little girl"—is El Niño's opposite. When seas along the equator in the eastern tropical Pacific are cold instead of warm and winds are strong instead of weak, La Niñas can cause climate havoc. La Niña is often not as powerful as her better-known brother, but she can still cause lasting chills, heavy rain, and severe storms. In 2011, a La Niña helped stir up one of the worst cyclones in Australia's history, with shrieking winds up to 285 kilometers (177 miles) per hour. Cyclone Yasi tore off roofs and snapped trees as thousands of Aussies had to evacuate their homes.

THE HAILSTORM that swept across France on July 13, 1788 brought hailstones so big that, according to one witness, they clobbered rabbits and killed partridge. They also helped ignite what many believe is among the most important events in human history—the French Revolution. A little over 200 years ago, farmers and other ordinary citizens in France banded together to demand food, fewer taxes, and more rights from their king. King Louis XVI was only the latest in a long line of French rulers who lived fabulously extravagant lives in glittering palaces while poor peasants huddled in dreary huts.

The hailstorm of 1788 began a series of bizarre weather events in Europe that researchers now believe were triggered by changes far away, in the Pacific Ocean. A severe El Niño was gathering momentum there, and for four years, it battered climates around the world, causing wild winds, storms, and crazy temperatures.

In France, the field-flattening hailstorm was followed by crop-killing droughts and bitter winters. Because rye, barley, and other grains had been destroyed by the harsh weather, a loaf of bread cost more than most people could pay. Desperate from cold and starvation, people began to riot and a revolutionary fever erupted. Before long, the king was overthrown and put on trial. In 1793, he, his queen, and thousands of French citizens lost their heads by the blade of a guillotine.

France formed a new kind of government, ruled by an assembly whose task was to represent all the people of France, not just the royal and the rich.

HA HA!

If a mountain blows his cool, should I grab my scarf and earmuffs?

IT'S NOT EASY making delicate clocks while wearing mitts.

Chauncey Jerome, a clockmaker in Connecticut, learned this lesson rather unexpectedly during the summer of 1816. In any other year, Jerome would have worked June 7 in his shirtsleeves, but that morning he put on his sweater. Then he put on his overcoat. Finally, he resorted to mittens. The late-spring weather was freezing.

Jerome had no way to know that the bizarre cold was just the beginning of what came to be known as "the year without summer." Ice covered New England rain barrels several times through the season. Quebec was blanketed by deep snow in June. And summer frosts across much of eastern North America killed corn and other crops before they could grow. In Europe, seemingly relentless rain and cold ruined harvests and caused a deadly famine.

Few people had ever heard of the Indonesian volcano known as Mount Tambora, which had erupted with a spectacular explosion half a world away and a whole year earlier. Tambora sent more ash and chemical vapors into the sky than any other eruption in the previous 500 years. The sulfur gas and other vapors floated in the Earth's upper atmosphere for more than a year, reflecting and scattering the sun's energy. Researchers believe the blast and its chilling gases were to blame for general cooling around the globe.

I'm so depressed.

SPOOKY TALES
Aargh! The famous horror story of *Frankenstein* is said to have been inspired by the dark and gloomy year that followed Mount Tambora's eruption.

Cool Music

If 17th-century instrument-maker Antonio Stradivari knew that some of his violins are now worth millions of dollars, he would have fallen off his stool. The Italian craftsman was rightly proud of his work, but these days, many musicians—and some wealthy collectors— consider Stradivarius violins to be better than any made before or since. Why? Part of the reason was a secret ingredient called climate.

Perfect!

The Little Ice Age was particularly frosty between 1645 and 1715, a time when Stradivari was at work in his northern Italian shop. According to researchers, the deep chill slowed the growth of forests in the nearby Alps. Stradivari used wood from those trees to make the tops of his instruments—the "sound board" that vibrates to help make music. The stunted trees meant dense, hard wood, ideal for creating the exquisite tone of the violins.

WHEN YOUR BUSINESS is nothing but bird droppings, you wouldn't expect climate change could actually make things worse. But in truth, bird guano (that is, poop) was a huge and profitable enterprise in Peru beginning about 170 years ago—or it was until El Niño showed up.

Bird feces are full of nitrogen and phosphorus, two chemicals important in plant fertilizers. The many seabird colonies along Peru's coast produced mountains of the stuff, and workers shoveled it onto ships for the gardens and farm fields of Europe and the United States. The droppings became the country's biggest export and soon made it rich.

But the prosperity was short-lived. In 1861, El Niño storms began battering the coast, killing millions of seabirds while washing away mountains of guano with torrential rains. The bird colonies—and the fertilizer industry—struggled to recover until another El Niño hit 16 years later. Again, the birds were devastated, and the Peruvian poop business finally went bust.

When Business Really Stinks

1821

We're free! Peru declares independence from Spain but the new country quickly realizes it's also broke.

1841

European traders smell opportunity: mountains of seabird poop cover tiny islands off Peru's shores, and the stuff makes great plant fertilizer.

1845

The age of guano has arrived. Peru gets "stinking" rich selling fowl feces to farmers in the United States and Europe.

1861

Whoosh! A severe El Niño dumps rain and waves over the poop mounds, washing lots of guano away and a few million birds too.

1877

Sploosh! Another mega El Niño strikes! The seabirds take another beating, and the poop is power-rinsed out to sea.

1880

The final scoop on the poop: Peru's guano business struggles but finds it's all washed up. The nation becomes poor again . . . but it smells better.

Watch out for the Bully

War is such a terrible thing that it's hard to imagine why anyone would start one. People who ponder the question point out that battles have often been about land, religion, or governments. According to scientists, however, climate sometimes picks a fight too.

Climate change can trigger flooding, famines, or droughts that cause conflicts between people left without land, food, or water and others who still have those things. Researchers who compared 500 years of climate information to 2,900 historic wars fought around the world between 1400 and 1900 found that fights broke out twice as often when the climate was cold and harsh than when it was mild and harvests were good.

Happens every time it snows.

QUESTION 38
Can you pin a medal on climate?

IN 1939, Adolf Hitler decided he wanted to make all of Europe into a single empire—*his* empire. He began marching the German army into neighboring countries. For the first two years of the Second World War, it looked as if Germany and its power-hungry friends might succeed. That was before climate joined the other side.

After successfully invading or taking control over most of its European neighbors, the German Army, with 3 million troops and thousands of tanks and airplanes, was stopped at the threshold of the Soviet capital of Moscow. The Soviet Red Army beat the enemy back—with considerable help from an ally called El Niño. Germany's failed attempt to take over the Soviet Union became a turning point in the war.

Researchers say an unusually bitter, cold winter helped repel the German attack on Moscow in 1941. The invaders were unprepared for the freezing temperatures and deep snow that scientists say was linked to a major El Niño on the other side of the planet. The climate event had begun in the eastern Pacific in the fall of 1939 and gathered strength through 1940 and 1941, affecting weather around the globe.

By the time Hitler's army reached the outskirts of Moscow, frigid temperatures and blizzards were waiting for them. The harsh cold, with frozen rain and sleet for variety, helped force the miserable German soldiers to retreat.

SOMETIMES
CLIMATE CHANGE
can lead to war, but war can
also lead to climate change. Scientists say that
the power of modern weapons can trigger lasting changes overhead.

In the 1991 Persian Gulf War, for example, more than 600 oil
wells in the country of Kuwait were set ablaze by Iraqi invaders.
The fires burned enough oil daily to fill millions of barrels and thick,
black smoke darkened the sky, blocking out the sun. Researchers say
the smoke made the region's climate cooler for months.

Nuclear weapons could have a far more lasting effect because of
gases and materials exploded high into the atmosphere. Scientists
estimate that the limited use of nuclear bombs in a small-scale war
would disrupt more people and cause more death by the resulting
effect on climate than by the bomb blasts or radioactive fallout.
Exploding fewer than 100 bombs—less than half a percent of the
world's total arsenal—would send enough gas and ash into the
atmosphere to transform the climate more profoundly than at any
other time in human history.

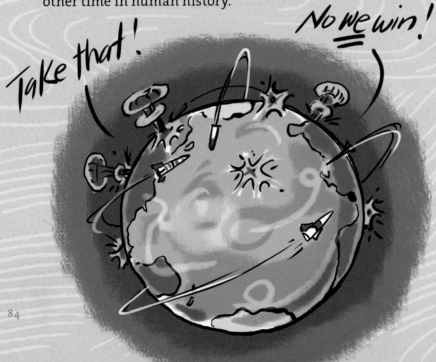

Clim-ACTivity:
THE MYSTERY OF THE ARTFUL ATMOSPHERE

The Scream by Edvard Munch is among the most recognized artworks in the world. The strange, howling figure with his hands at his face is a striking picture of human anguish. But the background adds to its power—a swirling red, orange, and yellow sunset. What might have inspired the artist to paint such a weird sky?

The clues: Researchers reviewed Munch's letters, and retraced the artist's steps around his hometown of Oslo, Norway, in the 1880s. They also noted that in late August 1883, an Indonesian volcano, Krakatau (also known as Krakatoa), erupted so violently it nearly blew apart its entire island.

Now just act naturally.

Although Krakatau exploded on the far side of the world, the sulfur gas and ashes it spewed not only changed the climate but also transformed the sunlight by acting like a prism. The researchers say the resulting spectacular sunsets likely inspired the painter.

CHAPTER 6

KEEPING our COOL

SO, IF CLIMATE HAS ALWAYS CHANGED, what's the big deal? Well, today's climate is changing faster than in the past 10,000 years, faster than any human civilization has witnessed before. And this time, people are behind it. To power our homes, our factories, and our cars, we humans are burning fuels that create carbon dioxide and other gases that trap heat from the sun. At the same time, we're changing the environment and cutting forests that help keep these gases in check.

Understanding the difference between today's global warming and the climate curveballs of the past is an important part of learning how to beat the future heat.

QUESTION 40
Who did it?
Watt did it?

JAMES WATT just wanted to make life easier. Watt was an 18th-century engineer, surveyor, instrument-maker, and inventor who lived in Scotland. In the 1760s, he improved the steam engine so that automated machines could do work once done entirely by humans, horses, or other beasts. Engine-powered machines were soon helping people to sew clothes, make toys, and even plow fields. Mechanized factories, gas-powered vehicles, and other contraptions made some jobs easier and much faster.

Historians call this change the Industrial Revolution, and most agree that it ended a lot of back-breaking labor and paved the way for the astonishing progress of the past 200 years.

There was one hitch that Watt probably didn't think of, though. Engines burn coal, oil, or gas to make them go—and this releases carbon dioxide and other greenhouse gases. As more factories are built and more cars take to the world's roads, the downside of Watt's idea is adding to an upswing in temperatures.

Climate Detectives Crack the Case

If the favorite tool of a detective is a magnifying glass, the instrument of choice for climate sleuths is the thermometer.

Thermometers have shown that the decade between 2000 and 2010 included nine of the Earth's hottest years since records began 150 years ago. Most of the warmest years since your granny's granny's *granny* was alive have happened since you were born.

To crack the climate case, scientists have gathered thousands of clues from the past. Growth rings from ancient trees, prehistoric air bubbles caught deep in glacier ice, and fossilized mud and minerals from lake bottoms and sea beds all help reveal our climate's shifty history.

The verdict? In the last 50 years, the Earth's northern half was hotter on average than it has been in more than 500 years. Scientists also think it was warmer than the past 1,300 years, but the evidence is less precise that far back. Most researchers agree that no natural cause—such as volcanoes, changes in our orbit, or sunspots—can explain why we are heating up so fast now. The only remaining suspect, say the detectives, is us.

QUESTION 41
If it's so hot,
why am I NOT?

A FIERCE 2010 SNOWSTORM dumped a record amount of snow on Washington, DC, and was dubbed "Snow-mageddon" or "SnOMG" as it swept across much of the eastern United States and Canada. Beijing, meanwhile, had its coldest morning in almost 40 years and its biggest snowfall since 1951. In the same year, Britain saw its longest cold snap since 1981, and then, in 2011, northern Mexico reported record low temperatures.

"Global *warming*?" say some. "Who are you kidding?"

Crazy weather is confusing. So are reports we sometimes hear about climate scientists being wrong. In 2007, a leading international research group reported that global warming would cause all the glaciers in the Himalaya Mountains of Nepal to melt within three decades. A few months later, the researchers said the claim was a mistake.

BLOWHARD
Warmer doesn't always mean nicer. The hottest year on record, 2005, was the year Hurricane Katrina pummeled New Orleans. Scientists believe warmer surface water in the Atlantic makes hurricanes more powerful.

Strange weather reports are not unexpected, because climate is the general weather picture of a place over a long time. With our current climate pattern, say scientists, the weather will become generally warmer, but will also be unpredictable. Zany storms—including extremely cold and snowy ones—will happen more often.

And scientific mistakes do happen, such as the prediction of the total Himalayan glacier melt. But the vast majority of scientists around the world now have no doubt that we have a problem: gases from our factories, electricity stations, and vehicles are warming our world more quickly than ever before. Arguing wastes time we could use to figure out smarter ways for humans to live on our only planet.

IT'S THE ATTACK OF THE KILLER COWS! *Billions of 'em! And they're going to burp us to a crisp!*

Cows have been taking a lot of heat recently, and it's because of their constant belching and flatulence. The problem is not so much their lack of manners, though. Every little burp and fart contains methane gas. Methane is a greenhouse gas and, like carbon dioxide, it prevents heat energy from escaping our atmosphere. Although carbon dioxide created by people has a much greater impact, methane (less common but with over 20 times the warming power of carbon dioxide) is a growing problem.

Roughly 1.4 billion domestic cattle live and burp around the world, almost 100 million more than there were just 20 years ago. That's one cow for every five people, thanks to the human appetite for beef, cheese, butter, milk, yogurt, and leather for shoes, furniture, and more. All those belching cattle produce about one-sixth of the methane released into the air each year. According to one study, the methane produced by cows, goats, sheep, and horses in the United States alone contributed as much to global warming in one year as the tailpipe exhaust from 33 million cars and trucks—about one-sixth of all cars driving on American roads.

Cow Gas = Car Gas

QUESTION 43
Do you sea what I see?

OCEANS PROBABLY DON'T mean to throw their weight around. But when you are as big as the combined force of the world's massive seas, you have a lot of influence. That's why, despite all the changes happening overhead, climate scientists spend time looking down at the water.

Oceans wash over 70 percent of the planet's surface. They float fleets and provide fish to millions of people who live along their coasts. They also move heat around the globe with their currents. And in the last 50 years, the world's oceans have become warmer far down into their dark depths. Like other substances, water expands when it is warm because heat spurs molecules to move and collide, shifting them away from each other. Because warmer water takes up more room and oceans are also filling with water from melting polar glaciers, sea levels are rising.

Each year, the world's oceans creep higher by an amount equal to the width of your baby fingernail. That may not seem like much, but many scientists say that the rate is increasing, and that within your lifetime, sea levels could be above your waist or higher. That would be enough to flood many coastal cities, including New York, New Orleans, and Shanghai.

ALL WET
In the Maldives, an island nation, politicians donned scuba gear to hold a meeting underwater. Rising seas are a big worry—most of the islands are less than 2 meters (6.6 feet) above sea level.

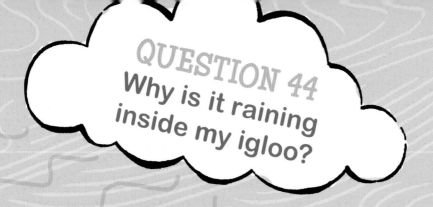
THE ARCTIC IS CHAMPION when it comes to losing its cool—the climate there is warming twice as fast as the planet generally. Scientists say the region is absorbing far more of the sun's heat than it used to because there's less ice and snow.

Snow and ice don't cool air the way ice cubes cool a drink, but work more like an enormous mirror. They reflect sunlight off their white surfaces and send it back into space. As snow melts, leaving dark earth, or as ice covering the deep-blue ocean shrinks, energy from the sun is absorbed as heat. That sends temperatures climbing higher, causing even more melting and, in turn, more warming.

A lot of tundra that used to be permanently frozen, known as perma-frost, is getting soft, causing roads and buildings to literally sink into the ground. At sea, ice covering the Arctic Ocean has been shrinking dramatically. Some scientists think the summertime ocean might be completely ice-free by 2030.

ICY DIP
The water pouring into the ocean from the huge melting ice sheets over Antarctica could fill as many as 60 million Olympic-sized swimming pools every year.

yay!

QUESTION 45
Can they bear it?

POLAR BEARS ARE COOL. The world's largest land-dwelling hunter—twice as large as a Siberian tiger—strolls the ice around the Arctic Circle looking for a good seal meal, and otherwise taking life easy.

But things are getting hot for the chilled-out bears. Only about 22,000 of the lumbering white predators live in the Arctic today, and researchers say rising temperatures threaten to cut their population by a third to two-thirds within the next 40 years. That's because these great bears need sea ice to be able to hunt seals, a fatty meal that's central to their diet, and the ice is melting fast. Finding their primary food will become more and more difficult.

Polar bears have become a symbol for worried wildlife watchers, because cold-loving animals are the first to feel the heat and have fewer coping options. But climate change is global, and research suggests up to a third of plants and animals worldwide could risk extinction by 2100 if greenhouse gases keep climbing.

BLOG FOG

Smart phones, iPads, and PCs are amazing fountains of information, but producing or running them also spews greenhouse gases into the atmosphere. Today's computer industry creates about the same amount of the climate-changing gases as all the passenger and cargo planes around the world.

Topped Out

Pikas are furry animals with bunny faces and oversized mouse ears. They look more adorable than tough, but these cousins of rabbits survive on some of the world's harshest, most windswept and frigid mountaintops. They prefer it that way because their body heat runs high.

But scientists say many pikas are now in trouble. Warmer temperatures are creeping up mountainsides, and areas of alpine cold are shrinking. Pikas can't dial down their thermostat, and they overheat in temperatures most people would enjoy.

Warming habitats are forcing many animals and plants to change where they live. A study of 99 birds, butterflies, and mountain plants found that, every 10 years, these species moved northward (or upward, on mountainsides) by the distance of a two-hour hike.

Other animals and plants have changed *how* they live. Many are getting the jump on spring's earlier arrival by shifting their springtime activities, such as nesting or blossoming, by a few days. Species that find ways to go with the flow are more likely to survive in a rapidly changing world.

AHH!

ice cream

PEAS

NEVER MIND DRAGONS. The real danger to damsels is climate change. Damselfish are small, often brilliant blue or yellow fish that live in colorful coral reefs. But coral—the tiny marine organisms responsible for creating the world's vast, beautiful coral reefs—is in deep trouble because of a one-two punch by global warming.

Corals host tiny algae that give them food and also their color. When stressed by too much warmth or cold, or when the water becomes too acidic, many corals expel their algae and "bleach" out their color. Scientists say more carbon dioxide from factories and cars is not only warming the ocean, the gas is also being absorbed by water, affecting the chemistry of oceans and making them more acidic. The result is more dead coral and more coral without color.

Like other reef fish, damselfish count on the bright coral to make their own colorful attire less obvious. But in a bleached-out environment, the damsels stick out like clowns in the desert. An experiment used aquariums with either bleached or non-bleached coral, and scientists discovered that damselfish were more likely to be eaten by other fish when the coral around them was white.

The damsels are not alone in their distress: many coral species are in hot water. Recently, a study of almost 300 species of Caribbean reef fish found that fishy numbers had fallen by one-third to three-quarters between 1996 and 2007. Disappearing coral, say the researchers, appears to be the most likely cause.

uh oh!

It's a nerd!
It's a plane!

Is it a bird? Is it a plane? Is it a scientist wearing a cape?

GLOBAL WARMING is not the only recent problem the world has faced from the sky. Thirty-five years ago, a young scientist named Jonathan Shanklin became an unexpected hero by jumping to the rescue when the world's sky had a dangerous hole in it.

Shanklin was not long out of university when he led the discovery by a British research team of an "ozone hole" over Antarctica. The "hole" was actually an unusual thinness in a layer of air, rich in a gas called ozone, that circles the globe high in the upper atmosphere. Shanklin and his colleagues blamed it on laboratory-produced chemicals used in spray cans, air conditioners, and refrigerators. The discovery frightened people because ozone protects us (and everything else) from 90 percent of the sun's cancer-causing ultraviolet rays.

Shanklin's story is worth remembering when we wonder whether the world is capable of tackling the problem of global warming. Back then, refrigerator-makers were determined to keep using the ozone-damaging chemicals, but within two years of Shanklin's discovery, an international meeting in Montreal banned the chemicals altogether in countries around the planet.

SOMETIMES FIGHTING GLOBAL WARMING can be downright dirty work—just ask the whales whose giant-sized poop is actually helping to reduce greenhouse gases.

Scientists say the almost 12,000 sperm whales living and pooping in southern oceans are helping the sea absorb a significant amount of carbon dioxide. Iron in the whale feces helps fertilize billions of tiny, free-floating plants called phytoplankton and they, in turn, suck up as much as 360,000 tonnes (400,000 tons)—equal to the weight of about 20 aircraft carriers—of carbon dioxide through photosynthesis every year. The system works because the whales feed on squid in the dark of the deep sea but swim near the sunlit surface to defecate, transferring nutrients out of the inky depths up to where plants can use them.

Still, whale waste helps the oceans absorb only a small fraction of the greenhouse gases poured into our atmosphere every year by factories and cars. Perhaps more important, the toilet-time work of whales is a good reminder that Nature still has a few tricks up her sleeve when it comes to managing climate. Taking care of our planet and protecting animals can have surprising benefits that are hard to imagine before their interconnections are revealed.

Just doing my bit to save the planet.

QUESTION 49
Are you warming up our world right now?

IF A LAMP is helping you read this book, chances are that some of its electricity comes from a generating plant that sends carbon dioxide into the air. Most of us don't notice many of the things we do that create greenhouse gas. They're just part of our everyday lives—things such as watching television, opening the refrigerator, or working and playing on computers.

More than a third of all the carbon dioxide North Americans pour into the sky comes from powering our homes. Our houses are bigger than those in many other places, and we have more machines that use up energy. In fact, American homes alone create close to 10 percent of all greenhouse gases in the world. That's more than the total amount produced by any nation except China.

Our North American appetite for energy may sound bad, but it actually means that we can make a big difference by making some changes in our lives. Recently, researchers calculated what would happen if just one-third of people in the United States changed their habits. They found that homeowners would likely cut greenhouse gases within 10 years by an amount equal to what all of France produces now.

Many steps we can take to lower our impact are simple—shutting off lights, televisions, and computers when we leave a room, turning down thermostats at night, line-drying our clothes, and taking shorter showers. We could ask our parents to use air conditioners less often, and tell them we'd rather bus or bike than drive to soccer practice.

It almost sounds too easy, but it works—and home is the perfect starting place for efforts to help the climate.

STEPWISE
A carbon footprint isn't a mark you leave on the rug. It refers to the amount of greenhouse gas something or someone releases into the air.

Stinky Chic

It's not dirt, it's earth!

Maybe one day it'll be cool to stink. As more people get wise to the causes of climate change, it could become fashionable to show you're doing your part—and what more obvious way than a little *eau de nature* body odor to signal that you're taking fewer showers?

If you want to be noticed more for your strong character or talents than your strong smell, though, shortening shower time would be a smart move. Homes account for more than a third of greenhouse gases, and about a third of home power use is from heating water. Using less hot water—not just in showers, but for washing dishes and clothes too—can make a difference.

Clim-ACTivity:

THE CASE OF THE TRAVELING TOMATO

VIP LOUNGE

Did your tomato sail here? How pampered were those grapes before they arrived in your refrigerator? In summer, fruits and vegetables grow close to home, but during winter, many come to us from far corners of the planet. So how do you pick a climate-friendly menu?

The Tomato Challenge:

A nice tomato slice is delicious in a sandwich, but in many places winter makes growing the fruit outdoors impossible. Heated greenhouses produce out-of-season tomatoes close to home, but create carbon dioxide and other greenhouse gases. On the other hand, tomatoes grown year round in warm climates may be sent to us in container ships, trucks, and even planes that generate gases as they make their way north. Which tomato would you choose?

ANSWER

A well-traveled tomato is actually better. A study in England found that winter tomatoes sent by ship from sunny Spain were responsible for fewer greenhouse gas emissions than tomatoes grown in local, heated greenhouses. In the United States, 80 percent of all greenhouse gases produced while getting food to the table was created in the growing phase, while about 15 percent was generated through shipping and delivery.

CONCLUSION

WONDERING WEATHER

ONE CONFUSING THING about climate is that we can't see it. That can make it hard to imagine how climate change could be such a big deal.

But climate *is* a big deal. It decides whether today's weather will be what we expect it to be. Climate is important to wildlife because reliable weather is often vital to their survival. It's important to us too, because it affects where we live, grow food, or find fresh water. It even helps people get along with one another. If climate changes, these things may change too.

QUESTION 50
What would the Egyptians do?

LUCKY FOR US, people are ingenious creatures. Consider the ancient Egyptians. When a massive drought caused a famine that eventually toppled the Old Kingdom of the pharaohs 4,200 years ago, local Egyptians took matters into their own hands. They began digging ditches.

Starting with simple channels to carry water from the dwindling Nile, some Egyptian settlements developed complex irrigation systems and reservoirs to save their thirsty crops. The ancient Egypt of the pharaohs never recovered, but a new Egyptian kingdom emerged and carried on for another 2,000 years. Egyptian know-how saved the day.

From our early days, humans have been good at finding answers to questions—even tough questions like "What do we do now?" By searching for solutions, we're finding ways to respond to a changing climate and ways to cut greenhouse gases. Human curiosity has always been our most valuable tool. The key to coping with global warming might be global wondering: knowing more makes all the difference.

Not as impressive as a pyramid, but more useful.

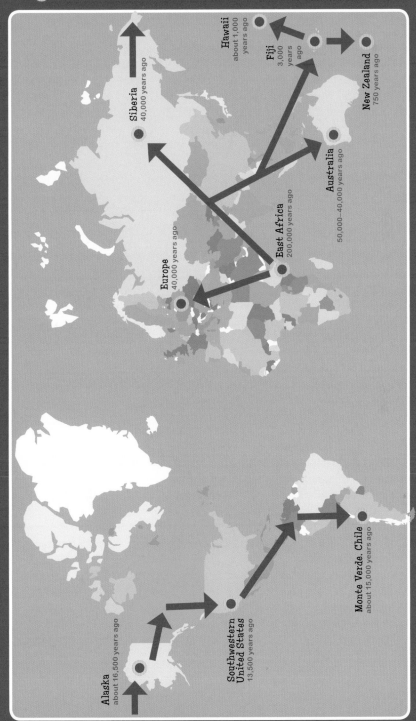

FURTHER READING

Adams, Simon, and Katherine Baxter. *The Kingfisher Atlas of the Ancient World*. New York: Kingfisher Publishing, 2006.

Amsel, Sheri. *Everything Kids' Environment Book: Learn How You Can Help the Environment—By Getting Involved at School, at Home, or at Play (Everything Kids Series)*. Avon, MA: Adams Media, 2007.

Arnold, Caroline. *El Niño: Stormy Weather for People and Wildlife*. New York: Clarion Books, 2007.

Christie, Peter. *The Curse of Akkad: Climate Upheavals That Rocked Human History*. Toronto: Annick, 2008.

Cole, Joanna, and Bruce Degen. *The Magic School Bus and the Climate Challenge*. New York: Scholastic, 2010.

Corrick, James A. *Early Middle Ages (World History)*. San Diego: Lucent, 2005.

David, Laurie, and Cambria Gordon. *The Down-to-Earth Guide to Global Warming*. New York: Scholastic, 2007.

Desonie, Dana. *Climate (Our Fragile Planet)*. New York: Chelsea House, 2007.

DK Publishing. *Early Humans (DK Eyewitness Books)*. New York: DK Books, 2005.

Evans, Kate. *Weird Weather: Everything You Didn't Want to Know about Climate Change But Probably Should Find Out*. Toronto: Groundwood Books, 2007.

Fradin, Dennis, and Judith Fradin. *Witness to Disaster: Volcanoes*. Washington: National Geographic Children's Books, 2007.

Furgang, Kathy. *Tambora: A Killer Volcano from Indonesia (Volcanoes of the World)*. New York: PowerKids Press, 2001.

Guiberson, Brenda, and Chad Wallace. *Earth: Feeling the Heat*. New York: Henry Holt, 2010.

Hall, Julie, and Sarah Lane. *A Hot Planet Needs Cool Kids: Understanding Climate Change and What You Can Do About It*. Washington: Green Goat Books, 2008.

Holmes, Thom. *Early Humans: The Pleistocene and Holocene Epochs (The Prehistoric Earth)*. Philadelphia: Chelsea House, 2008.

Hynson, Colin. *Elizabeth I and the Spanish Armada (Stories from History)*. Grand Rapids, MI: School Specialty Publishing, 2006.

Lourie, Peter. *The Lost World of the Anasazi: Exploring the Mysteries of Chaco Canyon*. Honesdale, PA: Boyds Mills Press, 2003.

Mattern, Joanne. *Leif Eriksson: Viking Explorer (Explorers!)* Berkeley Heights, NJ: Enslow, 2004.

Miller, Lee. *Mystery of the Lost Colony (Roanoke)*. New York: Scholastic, 2007.

Morgan, Sally, and Jenny Vaughan. *Climate Change (Earth SOS)*. London: Franklin Watts, 2007.

Perl, Lila. *The Ancient Maya (People of the Ancient World)*. London: Franklin Watts, 2005.

Peters, Stephanie True. *The Black Death (Epidemic!)*. New York: Benchmark Books, 2004.

Ripperton, Lisa, and Ellwood W. Kemp. *Streams of History: Early Civilizations*. Chapel Hill, NC: Yesterday's Classics, 2008.

Seibert, Patricia. *Discovering El Niño: How Fable and Fact Together Help Explain the Weather*. Markham, ON: Fitzhenry & Whiteside, 2004.

Seymore, Simon. *Global Warming*. New York: Harper Collins Children's Books, 2010.

Sloan, Christopher. *The Human Story: Our Evolution from Prehistoric Ancestors to Today*. Washington, DC: National Geographic Children's Books, 2004.

Spilsbury, Louise A. *Changing Climate: Living with the Weather*. Eustis, FL: Raintree, 2006.

Tanaka, Shelley. *Climate Change*. Toronto: Groundwood Books, 2006.

Thornhill, Jan. *This Is My Planet: The Kids' Guide to Global Warming*. Toronto: Maple Tree Press, 2010.

Tyldesley, Joyce. *Egypt (Insiders)*. New York: Simon & Schuster Children's Publishing, 2007.

Unwin, Mike. *Climate Change*. Chicago: Heinemann, 2006.

Woodward, John. *Climate Change (DK Eyewitness Books)*. New York: DK Books, 2008.

SELECTED BIBLIOGRAPHY

CHAPTER 1

Chyba, C.F. "Rethinking Earth's Early Atmosphere." *Science* 308 (2005): 962–63.

Grasby, S.E., H. Sanei, and B. Beauchamp. "Catastrophic Dispersion of Coal Fly Ash into Oceans during the Latest Permian Extinction." *Nature Geoscience* 4 (2011): 104–7.

Hoffman, P.F., and D.P. Schrag. "The Snowball Earth Hypothesis: Testing the Limits of Global Change." *Terra Nova* 14 (2002): 129–55.

Lacis, A.A., et al. "Governing Earth's Temperature Atmospheric CO2: Principal Control Knob." *Science* 330 (2010): 356–59.

Pain, S. "A Discovery in Need of a Controversy." *New Scientist*, May 16, 2009: 46–48.

Qiu, J. "A Trip to Dinosaur Time." *Nature* 467 (2010): 150–51.

Schulte, P., et al. "The Chicxulub Asteroid Impact and Mass Extinction at the Cretaceous-Paleogene Boundary." *Science* 327 (2010): 1214–18.

Smith, F.A., et al. "The Evolution of Maximum Body Size of Terrestrial Mammals." *Science* 330 (2010): 1216–19.

CHAPTER 2

Ambrose, S.H. "Late Pleistocene Human Population Bottlenecks, Volcanic Winter, and Differentiation of Modern Humans." *Journal of Human Evolution* 34 (1998): 623–51.

Begun, D.R. "Planet of the Apes." *Scientific American* 289 (2003): 74–83.

Bobe, R., A.K. Behrensmeyer, and R.E. Chapman. "Faunal Change, Environmental Variability and Late Pliocene Hominin Evolution." *Journal of Human Evolution* 42 (2002): 475–97.

Dalton, R. "Fossil Rewrites Early Human Evolution." *Nature* 461 (2009): 705–6.

deMenocal, P.B. "Climate and Human Evolution." *Science* 331 (2011): 540–42.

Grine, F.E., J.G. Fleagle, and R.E. Leakey, eds. *The First Humans: Origin and Early Evolution of the Genus* Homo, *Vertebrate Paleobiology and Paleoanthropology*. New York: Springer Science, 2009.

Lieberman, D.E. "Homing in on Early Homo." *Nature* 441 (2007): 291–92.

CHAPTER 3

Balter, M. "Ancient Algae Suggest Sea Route for First Americans." *Science* 320 (2008): 729.

Fagan, B. *The Long Summer: How Climate Changed Civilization*. New York: Basic Books, 2004.

Fitzhugh, W.W., and E.I. Ward, eds. *Vikings: The North Atlantic Saga*. Washington: Smithsonian Institution Press, 2000.

Goebel, T., M.R. Waters, and D.H. O'Rourke. "The Late Pleistocene Dispersal of Modern Humans in the Americas." *Science* 319 (2008): 1497–1502.

McGovern, T.H. "The Archaeology of the Norse North Atlantic." *Annual Review of Anthropology* 19 (1990): 331–51.

Mellars, P. "Why Did Modern Human Populations Disperse from Africa ca. 60,000 Years Ago? A New Model." *PNAS* 103 (2006): 9381–86.

Nunn, P.D., et al. "Times of Plenty, Times of Less: Last-millennium Societal Disruption in the Pacific Basin." *Human Ecology* 35 (2007): 385–401.

Stahle, D.W., et al. "The Lost Colony and Jamestown Droughts." *Science* 280 (1998): 564–67.

CHAPTER 4

Behringer, W. "Climatic Change and Witch-hunting: The Impact of the Little Ice Age on Mentalities." *Climatic Change* 43 (1999): 335–51.

Büntgen, U., et al. "2500 Years of European Climate Variability and Human Susceptibility." *Science* 331 (2011): 578.

deMenocal, P.B. "Cultural Responses to Climate Change during the Late Holocene." *Science* 292 (2001): 667–73.

Fagan, B. *The Little Ice Age: How Climate Made History, 1300–1850*. New York: Basic Books, 2000.

Linden, E. *The Winds of Change: Climate, Weather, and the Destruction of Civilizations*. New York: Simon and Schuster, 2006.

Muro, M. "New Site Suggests Anasazi Exodus." *Science* 290 (2000): 914–15.

Peterson, L.C., and G.H. Haug. "Climate and the Collapse of Maya Civilization: A Series of Multi-year Droughts Helped To Doom an Ancient Culture." *American Scientist* 93 (2005): 322–30.

Weiss, H. "Desert Storm." *The Sciences*. May/June 1996: 30–36.

CHAPTER 5

Brönnimann, S., et al. "Extreme Climate of the Global Troposphere and Stratosphere in 1940–42 Related to El Niño." *Nature* 431 (2004): 971–74.

Caviedes, C.N. *El Niño in History: Storming Through the Ages*. Gainesville, FL: University Press of Florida, 2001.

Diamond, J. *Collapse: How Societies Choose to Fail or Succeed*. London: Penguin Books, 2005.

Durschmied, E. *The Weather Factor: How Nature Has Changed History*. London: Hodder & Stoughton, 2000.

Fagan, B. *Floods, Famines, and Emperors: El Niño and the Fate of Civilizations*. New York: Basic Books, 1999.

Grove, R. "Global Impact of the 1789–93 El Niño." *Nature* 393 (1998): 318–19.

Kumar, K.K., et al. "Unraveling the Mystery of Indian Monsoon Failure during El Niño." *Science* 314 (2006): 115–19.

Olson, D.W. "When the Sky Ran Red: The Story behind *The Scream*." *Sky & Telescope* 107 (2004): 29–35.

Stommel, H.M., and E. Stommel. *Volcano Weather: The Story of 1816, the Year without a Summer*. New York: Simon & Schuster, 1983.

Zhang, D.D., et al. "Climate Change and War Frequency in Eastern China over the Last Millennium." *Human Ecology* 35 (2007): 403–14.

CHAPTER 6

Bradshaw, W.E., and C.M. Holzapfel. "Evolutionary Response to Rapid Climate Change." *Science* 312 (2006): 1477–78.

Desrochers, A. "The Prospects for Polar Bears." *Nature* 468 (2010): 905–6.

Flannery, T. *The Weather Makers*. Toronto: HarperCollins, 2005.

Kerr, R.A. "Global Warming Is Changing the World." *Science* 316 (2007): 188–90.

Krajick, K. "All Downhill from Here?" *Science* 303 (2004): 1601–3.

Mitchell, J.G., et al. "Iron Defecation by Sperm Whales Stimulates Carbon Export in the Southern Ocean." *Proceedings of the Royal Society B* 277 (2010): 3527–31.

Paddack, M.J., et al. "Recent Region-wide Declines in Caribbean Reef Fish Abundance." *Current Biology* 19 (2009): 590–95.

Parry, M.L., et al., eds. *Contribution of Working Group II to the Fourth Assessment Report of the Intergovernmental Panel on Climate Change, 2007*. New York: Cambridge University Press, 2007.

Shanklin, J. "Reflections on the Ozone Hole." *Nature* 465 (2010): 34–35.

Weaver, A.J. *Keeping Our Cool: Canada in a Warming World*. Toronto: Penguin Canada, 2010.

Willis, K.J., and S. Bhagwat. "Biodiversity and Climate Change." *Science* 326 (2009): 806–7.

INDEX

ACKNOWLEDGMENTS

I'm grateful to Dr. Thomas Pedersen, executive director of the Pacific Institute for Climate Solutions at the University of Victoria, for his review of the material in this book and for his comments and suggestions. Once again, I'm very thankful for the patient work of Elizabeth McLean, a champion editor. I would also like to thank Ross Kinnaird and everyone at Annick. As always, my final note of gratitude is for Priscilla, Hannah, and Laura for their wonderful support.

IMAGE CREDITS

ABOUT THE AUTHOR

Peter Christie frequently writes about climate change. His book for teens, *The Curse of Akkad: Climate Upheavals That Rocked Human History*, also describes catastrophic climate shifts through time. His other books for children, *Animal Snoops, Naturally Wild Musicians*, and *Well-Schooled Fish and Feathered Bandits*, explore the science of animal behavior. He lives in Kingston, Ontario, with his wife and their two young daughters.

ABOUT THE ILLUSTRATOR

Ross Kinnaird has illustrated over 25 books for children. When asked how he comes up with his ideas, he replies that he sits in a bath of warm lemonade with a frozen chicken on his head!

The thing he enjoys most about being an illustrator is visiting schools to talk about books and drawing funny pictures of teachers. He has been to about 150 schools and spoken to thousands of kids.

He loves to travel and has visited Australia, Israel, Morocco, and countries throughout Asia and Europe.

If you like asking questions, check out these other books in the 50 QUESTIONS series:

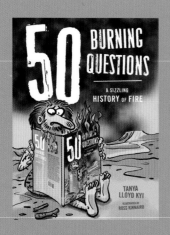 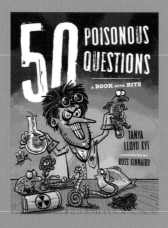 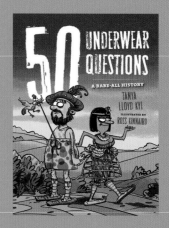

50 BURNING QUESTIONS: A Sizzling History of Fire
by Tanya Lloyd Kyi, illustrated by Ross Kinnaird
paperback $12.95 | hardcover $21.95

"(A) lighthearted, informative look at a fascinating subject ... Accessibly written and appealingly designed . . ."
— *KIRKUS REVIEWS*

". . . a fun and informative book for anyone fascinated by fire, which means pretty much everyone."
— *BOOKLIST*

50 POISONOUS QUESTIONS: A Book with Bite
by Tanya Lloyd Kyi, illustrated by Ross Kinnaird
paperback $12.95 | hardcover $21.95

". . . just the thing to entice readers seeking intriguing facts."
— *SCHOOL LIBRARY JOURNAL*

". . . easy to understand writing and humorous illustrations . . . make 50 POISONOUS QUESTIONS fun as well as educational. Highly recommended."
— *CM MAGAZINE*

50 UNDERWEAR QUESTIONS: A Bare-All History
by Tanya Lloyd Kyi, illustrated by Ross Kinnaird
paperback $12.95 | hardcover $21.95

Underwear has played a role in ancient crusades, city sieges, and even modern economic predictions. Obviously, it's time to uncover the facts about everything from loincloths and T-shirts to bloomers and lingerie. Young readers will laugh their pants off at the accompanying cartoons and get the bare, but fascinating, facts about the history of our unmentionables.